Good Morning Children

Devotional Teachings from a Mother's Heart

SANDRA MAE EHRGOTT

WESTBOW
PRESS®
A DIVISION OF THOMAS NELSON
& ZONDERVAN

Scriptures taken from the Holy Bible, New International Version®, NIV®. Copyright © 1973, 1978, 1984, 2011 by Biblica, Inc.™ Used by permission of Zondervan. All rights reserved worldwide. www.zondervan.com The "NIV" and "New International Version" are trademarks registered in the United States Patent and Trademark Office by Biblica, Inc.™ All rights reserved.

Scripture taken from the King James Version of the Bible.

WestBow Press books may be ordered through booksellers or by contacting:

WestBow Press
A Division of Thomas Nelson & Zondervan
1663 Liberty Drive
Bloomington, IN 47403
www.westbowpress.com
1 (866) 928-1240

ISBN: 978-1-4908-8429-5 (sc)
ISBN: 978-1-4908-8430-1 (hc)

Print information available on the last page.

WestBow Press rev. date: 01/20/2016

Dedication

To my Lord and Savior, Jesus Christ, for without Him I am nothing. He is the inspiration of my thoughts and writings in this book. Words cannot express my gratitude for the guidance He gives to my life each day.

May the words of these pages bring Him Glory and inspire us always to live a life worthy of the life we have been given.

I love you Lord!

Sandra Mae

Foreword
"The Noble Woman"

"A wife of noble character who can find? She is worth more than rubies" (Proverbs 31:10 New International Version).

Who would rise early and stay up late, prayerfully crafting a heartfelt message of encouragement each day to children who had long since left her home and started families of their own? A noble woman would! Who would voluntarily ask to take her grandchildren frequently so her children could have a break, and so that she could impart spiritual realities into the lives of those grandchildren by leading them on serving expeditions, both domestic and international? A noble woman would!

Who would faithfully look after aging parents without complaining or expecting anything in return? And who would work side by side with her father in a family business continuing to offer support even when it was clear that the business needed to close? A noble woman would!

Who would encourage and support a husband who traveled frequently and who sometimes offered less than deserved appreciation for all the big and little things she did to manage and make their home beautiful and inviting? And who would do it all without complaining? A noble woman would! Who would gladly work odd jobs and contract work; turning her home into a cosmetology salon in order to earn much needed extra income? A noble woman would!

Who would faithfully accompany her spouse through the demands, difficulties and disappointments of life while insulating her children from harm throughout the process? A noble woman would!

And who would do it all out of gratitude as faithful service to the Lord she loves? A noble woman would!

I know; I married her!

Thanks to some friends who introduced me to spiritual disciplines early in my Christian experience, I learned the value of reading, memorizing and meditating on scripture passages. In the beginning, I would memorize topical passages that helped me deal with areas of struggle in my growth as a new believer. Topics like patience, temptation, thankfulness, and peace were the typical subjects of my early experiments into this lost art.

Then I found Proverbs. After spending a considerable amount of time in the beginning chapters of this book I became impatient. (I guess I should have spent a little more time in that area!) Consequently, I skipped to the back of Proverbs. That is where I found the "*Noble Woman*". Well, at least conceptually. I had discovered what seemed to be some amazing traits of what must represent the woman every man desired and what every woman aspired to become. Most importantly this is a woman even praised and affirmed by God as one "*who fears the Lord*" (Proverbs 31:30).

I became very familiar with this passage. I wanted to find a noble woman; and I thought it was important enough that I wanted to help other young men desire and identify a woman of this kind of character. I guess I was hoping there were enough of these kind of women to go around.

So as a young youth leader and student group worker, I developed an entire lesson aimed at instructing young men in desiring and identifying the characteristics of this amazing woman.

It is interesting how one can see so clearly spiritual truths and principles in God's Word and then fail to recognize those same things when they are lived out right in front of us. I have to admit that though I knew from Proverbs 31 what a noble woman was, I was deficient when it came to recognizing what a noble woman I had married. Oh, I knew from the beginning that she was special, unique, beautiful and talented. She was by all accounts a precious gift from God. In fact our meeting, courtship and marriage is a God story that is for another book.

I think part of the problem was that I was untrained in recognizing nobility; even though it was right with me all the time. Part of the beauty of the noble woman is how she unassumingly and humbly teaches those around her how to recognize her qualities.

Over the entire thirty-seven years of marriage, and especially the last few years since our children have been on their own, I have come to recognize the beauty of nobility in my amazing wife. I have watched her faithfully share with our children and our grandchildren the wisdom God has imparted to her through her relationship with Him.

There is a poem that was written many years ago by a man intending to praise his mother for all the qualities of motherhood she personified. The first line is as follows. *"'M' is for the many things she gave me..."* You may or may not know the rest. The point being that in acrostic fashion the author details the wonderful characteristics of this woman who was the consummate mother.

Proverbs 31:10-31 is an acrostic poem in which the Holy Spirit through this author articulates the many virtues of the noble woman; *"one who fears the Lord"*.

They include the virtues of a woman who inspires confidence in her husband and who works diligently; who serves the underserved in the streets without neglecting the needs and dreams of her own household; who lives life with an infectious trust in her God.

There are too many virtues to list here so let me just invoke the verse the author uses to summarize his thoughts.

"Her children arise and call her blessed; her husband also, and he praises her: 'Many women do noble things but you surpass them all!' Charm is deceptive and beauty is fleeting, but a woman who fears the Lord is to be praised" (Proverbs 31:28-30).

My wife is my Proverbs 31 woman. I am convinced of that, and every day I learn to appreciate her more. In her daily life I have seen her live out, with God's help, the virtues written in each stanza of this poem.

This book is a by-product of that life. It is the stuff of true nobility.

It wasn't written to be a book. Each portion was written as just that; a daily morsel or message of encouragement, warning, sympathy or as a personal need to vent her own frustration to her trusted audience. Those daily messages are compiled here for your edification and inspiration.

It was written from the heart of a mother who cares deeply about the well being of her family and is willing to sacrifice everything, even her own life, to ensure that they understand the Mother heart of God.

May you find encouragement, warning, sympathy and even permission to vent your own frustrations as you read this book.

A Grateful Husband,

Doug Ehrgott

Doug and Sandy

Son Christopher and Becky

Reflections

"As I open my inbox at work every day the first email that I look for is the one labeled, '*Good Morning Children*'. I know by seeing those words that my day will be better for it. I remember the first time that I saw it back in June of 2004, and wondered what it was. As I opened it up and read the words that my mom had written to me, I realized how truly blessed I was to have her as a mother. The way she incorporated God's teaching into everyday life experiences helped me to get through some rough patches in my own life. Ten years later she still inspires us and teaches me how to be a better Christian, husband, brother, father and son. I am so very excited that others will now be blessed by the words that have shaped me over the last ten years. I love my mother very much, and it is her love for others and the way she shows God's love that makes me proud to call her '*Mom*'. My hope is that as you read these stories to your children they may understand God's love and the love of a mother who greeted us every day with three simple words that changed our lives. '*Good Morning Children*.'"

Chris Ehrgott

"Sandy has included me in the '*Good Morning Children*' emails even prior to me marrying her son. This meant so much to me as it made me feel like more of a part of Sandy's family and God's family. Her daily emails remind me of God's teachings through Bible verses and stories. The real life stories and experiences have made me laugh and cry, but most importantly they have helped me to see how to live out the word of God in my own life. Sandy is a true inspiration of living God's word and sharing it with others all over the world and in her own family!"

Becky Ehrgott

Daughter Beverly and Jon
Children Addi, Ayla, Brody, Ben, Asher (in heaven) and Nathan

Reflections

"'*Good Morning Children*' is something that is too good not to share. God has spoken to me so many times through these devotions. Sandy is able to capture powerful teaching moments in life intertwined with the truth of the Bible, which have spoken to me at just the right time. Her love for Jesus Christ and the truth of His Word, along with her love for her family shines through in each devotion."

Jon Howery

"As a mother of five young children, the words '*Good Morning Children*' is often followed by, '*Make your bed,*' '*Eat your breakfast,*' '*Brush your teeth,*' and other such instructions. But who instructs the mother? In my case it is still my mom! '*Be patient,*' '*Be kind,*' '*Listen to the voice of the Lord,*' '*Honor your spouse,*' '*Love your children,*' '*Show love to those in need,*' ...etc. These are the new instructions that I receive from my mother and that we all need to hear. I am so thankful to have my mother's advice always waiting for me!"

Beverly Howery

Son Jason and Tammy
Children Norah and Gavin

Reflections

"My mom's words have always meant so much to me. They have always been used to inspire, teach, challenge and encourage me. Her voice has always reassured me of her love and showed me the importance of a relationship with God. Growing up I heard this voice every day.

As I have grown older, she continues to speak to me. She uses her writings to communicate her heart. When I started receiving her emails titled, *'Good Morning Children'* I had no clue how impactful they would prove to be. I know when I open them I will hear a familiar and loving voice. That voice is still inspiring, teaching, challenging and encouraging me daily. I couldn't be more grateful!"

Jason Ehrgott

"Sandy started writing, *'Good Morning Children'* around the time I was married. I remember thinking, *'Wow how amazing is this family that I married into that she would take the time each day to personally write to me.'* Through the years, Sandy's writings have encouraged and challenged me in the way I think and view God's kingdom. In my favorite entry, Sandy describes seeing my daughter's face as an infant walking through the door and through her dependency and pure trust, she could see God's kingdom shining through her. It taught me not what I could teach my children, but what I could learn from them and about God's love."

Tamara Ehrgott

Son Joshua and Kelsey
Daughter Joselyn

Reflections

"My mom has always been a person inspired by God to proactively search for the lost. She is a very busy woman! She loves to stay active and is involved in many different ministries as she enjoys showing God's love to others in very practical ways. She is always looking for new opportunities and searching for the next adventure to bless others' lives. One of her best ministries, in my opinion, is her dedication and love for family, and her desire to share God's teachings to us. Over the past several years, my mom has shared her life and thoughts through her emails to us each day entitled, '*Good Morning Children*'. These morning visions have challenged me to keep God at the center of my life and have shown me the importance of having communication and devotion with our Savior. It has also shown me that she deeply cares about the faith of her children and instilling the importance of God's presence in all of our lives. A few verses that make me think of this book and the inspiration that Mom gives to me to bring up my own children with are…

'These commandments that I give you today are to be on your hearts. Impress them on your children. Talk about them when you sit at home and when you walk along the road, when you lie down and when you get up. Tie them as symbols on your hands and bind them on your foreheads. Write them on the doorframes of your houses and on your gates' (Deuteronomy 6:6-9).

'Start children off on the way they should go, and even when they are old they will not turn from it' (Proverbs 22:6).

My mom has done an excellent job of staying obedient to these scriptures. '*Good Morning Children*' is an avenue for my Mom to express what is most important in the world, and it has had an everlasting impact on my life. I am sure it will have the same affect for many others who read these wisdoms. Through her readings I have learned more and more each day about not only what God has done in her life and the visions He has given to her, but also I have gotten discernment from the teachings that are provided to help guide me through my own life. Mom has always made it a mission to share the love of Christ and the deep impact He has had on changing her life and this book is a great testament to that.

Thanks for all of your love and insight Mom. I love you and am so proud of the light you shine in this world!"

Josh Ehrgott

"'*Good Morning Children*' is one of the most beautiful labors of love I have been a part of. My mother-in-law has created these precious treasures that have really given us the opportunity to see even deeper into her soul and faith life. Honesty and realness are just two of a multitude of gifts this beautiful author possesses. These letters expose her heart and intimate thoughts about our Lord and Savior, and her sincere desires for her family. I treasure the words she authors because I know they come from some of the deepest parts of her being. Through these letters, I have gained wisdom with the Word, a more profound understanding of Christ, and a love for my family that I did not realize could be stronger.

I am honored and blessed to be Sandy Ehrgott's daughter-in-law, and I am so proud to be able to call her Mama Ehrgs. She has loved me through good and bad, high times and low. She has simply, yet powerfully, loved me for me. I adore my mother-in-law; I truly do.

Of the many things I have learned from her, the most important is the challenge she has put forth towards my faith and relationship with Christ and how it pertains to my family and me.

Having a relationship with Jesus Christ is what gives us a solid basis in life. Friendships, work, family, marriage, and child-rearing are all opportunities we are given to exemplify the workings of the Lord. These relationships and times in life are our opportunities to embody the heart of Christ and hopefully bless and encourage others in doing so.

Psalm 24:1 says, '*The earth is the LORD's, and everything in it, the world, and all who live in it.*'

Everything is His! These letters have challenged me to try to live that out. Sandy gives real, tangible, relatable examples of how to live the kind of life that the Lord desires for each and every one of us. I pray that whoever has the chance to read '*Good Morning Children*' experiences a sense of true hope and encouragement through the Lord."

Kelsey Ehrgott

Acknowledgements

To Doug, my husband, for loving, supporting, and believing in me. Thank you for being my teacher and best friend. I love you!

To my children and grandchildren thank you for loving and sharing me with so many others. Being your mom and Nana has given me such great joy. I love you!

To my Mom and Dad thank you for loving and supporting me over the years. I love you both!

To my brothers and sister thank you for always having my back! Dan thank you for your constant encouragement to publish this book.

I love you all!

To Becky Kinney for all the hours you have invested in editing this book. It would never have happened without you! I love you!

To all my wonderful friends who have been so supportive through the years. I love you!

Thank you Sheri Felipe for your awesome work on the cover. I love you!

Introduction

There comes a season in every mother's life when she realizes her mothering days are over.

I was a stay at home mom. I laugh as I write that because anyone who knows me knows I am always busy and hardly ever stay at home. But wherever I went or whatever I did my children became a part of it. One of my greatest desires was to bring honor to my husband and raise our children to walk in the ways of the Lord. I loved being married and loved being a mother. I loved my children's friends and loved having a house full of laughter.

I remember when our oldest son, Chris, was getting ready to go off to college. On many days I found myself with my eyes full of tears. I was so happy for him and proud of the man he was becoming, but the thought of him leaving home was hard for me. It was a time of releasing him into the world. I knew he would do well, but I would miss not seeing him every day. At that time, I still had three kids at home and life was very busy.

Then one day, it was time for my last son to leave. He was getting married, and I recall being at the wedding shower. We were playing a game to see how well we all knew Josh. The first set of questions were about when he was young, and I knew all of the answers while no one else did. The second set of questions were about his college and dating years, and I realized I could not answer the majority of them.

On the way home, my eyes once again filled with tears as I realized that soon all of my children would be gone from our home. I was extremely happy for all of them and I did not want them to always live with me.

It was then that I knew it was for this very reason God gave them to me; so that one day I would release them.

I was proud that they all had grown to love God and had married spouses who did as well, but I began to see clearly that what I had been doing for the last thirty years was about to look very different.

I had a lot more time on my hands now, and I was able to work on developing a closer relationship with God. This pursuit was much more difficult in my child-rearing days.

As I read the scriptures, I was amazed at how many times mothers were mentioned, and how important their teachings were. Even Proverbs 31 was written by a mother to her grown son, and she was still giving him advice.

Proverbs 31:1-3 says, *"The sayings of King Lemuel – an inspired utterance his mother taught him. Listen, my son! Listen, son of my womb! Listen, my son, the answer to my prayers! Do not spend your strength on women, your vigor on those who ruin kings."*

In Proverbs 6:20, grown men were still admonished not to forsake their mother's teachings. Of these teachings they were told in verses 21-22, to *"bind them always on your heart; fasten them around your neck. When you walk, they will guide you; when you sleep, they will watch over you; when you awake, they will speak to you."*

It was during this time of pursing God further that I began to write to my grown children. I shared with them how much they were loved and also shared the things God was teaching me. I would begin most letters with the greeting, *"Good Morning Children"*.

This book is a collection of some of those writings. It is my prayer that you too will find encouragement and instruction from God's Word, and that this book will inspire everyone who reads it to stay connected as a family through intentional and meaningful ways.

Enjoy,

Sandra Mae

"Being Prosperous and Successful"

Great Morning Children,

Today is the day the Lord has made! It is great!

Most of us want to be Prosperous and Successful. That's why most of us get up and work so hard to gain the things we desire, right? But in the end most of us are worn out, unfulfilled and broke. This morning, Kids, I want you to listen to what I am about to share with you. With all the conviction that is in me I implore you to take note of the Lord's word.

Joshua 1:8, *"Keep this Book of the Law always on your lips; meditate on it day and night, so that you may be careful to do everything written in it. Then you will be prosperous and successful."*

Kids, God's word is life. If you are not in the habit of reading His word daily, I ask that you would trust me on this one and begin to read it each morning. Even if it is just a verse that you meditate on all day, it will sustain you when you encounter the trials of the day.

Being Prosperous and Successful is not about making money. It is about being a man or woman of integrity. When you have that, you are wealthy. If you only read God's word to get things, you will never receive the fullness God has for you. In Joshua 1:13 the Lord says He gives us rest. To me that is peace of mind knowing that the Lord is in control. Four times in this chapter the Lord reminded Joshua, *"to be strong and courageous"*. In one place he says *"very courageous"*. Kids, we are going to face all kinds of difficulties in our lives. We must, no we have to gain our strength from the Lord. His word in us gives us a place to stand and be courageous.

God is faithful! Open His word today and soak in His goodness. He longs to meet with each of us. My love for each of you does not even begin to come close to the love God has for each of you. His love is perfect.

Sincerely,

Your Mother

"What are the Right Things?"

Good Morning Children,

I was reading in Amos this morning. I started thinking about my worship to God. Has it become routine and birthed out of a habit, or am I truly worshipping God a fresh and new each day? Sometimes if we think we do all the presumed "RIGHT THINGS" they are acceptable to God. I go to church, sing the songs, tithe and fellowship with the saints, and give to the poor. Good things, huh? But…are they? Are they things I do to make myself acceptable?

The Lord is speaking in Amos 5:21-23, "*I hate, I despise your religious festivals; your assemblies are a stench to me. Even though you bring me burnt offerings and grain offerings, I will not accept them. Though you bring choice fellowship offerings, I will have no regard for them. Away with the noise of your songs! I will not listen to the music of your harps.*"

It wasn't what they did that was wrong. It was the way they did it. It was about them trying to approve themselves, to be good enough or to look good and it was not about God. Their conduct outside of all these things is what really showed what was in their heart. Kids, a life of worship to God is not just about Sunday morning, singing a song, or fellowshipping and giving. It is a life lived every moment in the presence of God. He alone is to receive Glory.

Once again, today's reading inspired me to remember that I only need the acceptance of God, no one else.

Be real, Kids, all the time!

Love you much,

Mom

"Peace"

Good Morning Children,

In life there will be things that happen that you will not understand. There will never be an answer to some of your "*Why's?*" or "*What ifs?*" Yesterday a good friend of mine, Sharon, lost her granddaughter. She drowned in a pond. She was only 18 months old, which is about the same age as Addi. I could not even imagine her pain. All of us can relate to how we would feel if something happened to Addi.

I am sure she wondered why. How could God allow this to happen? Kids, sometimes it is just how life is and life is hard and unpredictable at times. But in order to keep peace, our minds can't concentrate on the "Whys?" and "What ifs?" To do so is endless and stressful because there will be no answer. Rather, keep your minds fixed on Jesus. This will help you fight the battle in your minds. I have often thought our battles are won in our thought life. I am sure for Sharon and her daughter it is torture in their minds right now. Pray for them.

Try not to relive your pain over and over. It is bad enough the first time. Protect your mind. It has the power to make you crazy or keep you in peace. My prayer for you today is found in Philippians 4:7, *"And the peace of God, which transcends <u>all</u> understanding, will <u>guard your hearts and your minds</u> in Christ Jesus."*

Lord, I ask for your protection over my family.

Love,

Mom

"Confidence"

Good Morning Children,

Yesterday we celebrated Addi's 2nd birthday. She wanted to go down the slide into the pool and came to get me several times to help her. The more she did it the less scared she became until finally she was doing it on her own. Her confidence outgrew her fears!

The point is; the more she practiced the more she trusted. It is the same way when we go to God for help. We learn to put our confidence in Him, practice what He tells us, and soon we believe and trust as our fears disappear.

"Therefore everyone who hears these words of mine and puts them into practice is like a wise man who built his house on the rock. The rain came down, the streams rose, and the winds blew and beat against that house; yet it did not fall, because it had its foundation on the rock" (Matthew 7:24-25).

Kids, I pray that you would put God's Word into practice. That it would be your confidence in any type of trouble you face. Remember that He is there to hold you until you are sliding on your own, just as He is always there to catch you!

I love you,

Mom

"Love Letter"

Good Morning Children,

Remember the love letters you have received? I still have all the ones your dad wrote to me while he was in college. They are wonderful! They are filled with pictures, poems and expressions of his love for me. I remember running to the mailbox each day to get them and then reading them over and over. I don't get many of them anymore. I figure we are not apart, yet we still express our love to each other and share our lives together each day.

I thought Paul's letter was a "Love Letter" to his friends in Philippi. He addresses himself as a servant in Philippians 1:1. Anyone in love should be a servant to the one he loves, right? In verse 2, Paul shares a greeting and a blessing over them of *"grace and peace"*. Verse 3, he gives thanks for them. Verse 4, he prays for them with joy and goes on to say because of their relationship as Christians in verse 5. In verse 6, he encourages them and is confident that the work Christ has started in their lives will carry on until the day Jesus returns. Verse 7, an expression of his love: Is it right for me to feel this way about you? You have shared in every part of my life. God can testify how I long for all of you.

Yesterday at work I just began to let people I am in relationship with know that I loved them. *Hey Lori, I love you…Carolyn, I love you… Tammy, I love you…*etc. To which they responded, *"OK, what do you want?"* Or others said, *"Hey, I want some of that!"*

How often we forget to tell people they are loved and appreciated. When I got home and checked my mail, guess what? Beverly had sent me a simple phrase, *"I love you mom! I miss you!"* My eyes filled with tears and are filling again as I write because everyone likes to know, even if they do know. So, Kids, I end with a paraphrase of Philippians 1:1-8.

Grace and Peace be to all of you. I want you to know how I thank God every day and every time I remember you. I pray for you all each day with great joy. First that you all know God and we share that together. I am confident that in all we will face in this life, God who has begun a work in each of you will carry it on until the day we go to be with Him. Is it right for me to be so madly in love with you? Absolutely! There is never a time I do not hold each of you in my heart, for whether I am having a bad day, or I am busy at work, you are still there. I long for all of you to be together, for God has given me such a great affection for all of you. Because of His love, I know better how to love you.

Forever and ever, YOU are planted on my heart.

Love you all so much,

Mom

"Love Costs"

Good Morning Children,

Philippians 1:12-14

Have you ever thought about the fact that when you make a commitment to love, it costs you something? Why is that? Love is supposed to feel good, right? I remember telling a friend once that having children was one of the greatest joys in my life, yet at the same time children can break your heart right in two. But, love is never an issue. If I was ever to be put in a situation where it was my life or yours...I would chose death. Paul was facing this same thing. He was facing death. Why? Because He loved...

He loved Jesus so much that the most important thing in his life was to make sure others knew him as well (vs. 12). Everyone knew where he stood on this issue, even the guards knew why he was in jail (vs. 13) and because of his commitment to suffer for what he believed because of this, other Christians were encouraged to move forward in their faith, courageously and fearlessly (vs. 14).

One evening, Dad and I took out a man who was a Muslim. He was one of the men we supported to reach the Muslim people for Christ. He shared his story with us. He was a Christian, but he was not sharing his faith. He knew in his country he would be persecuted or killed for his belief in Jesus. One day the Lord spoke to him and told him to quit his very secure job and witness to the Muslims. His response? *"No!"* It took two years before he would yield his life to the will of God. Since that time he has been beaten and left for dead many times. In fact, when we were talking to him he was recovering from a crushed arm. I asked him this question. *"Aren't you afraid you'll die?" "No,"* he replied. *"I'd just go home to the Lord."* He went on to tell us that because he had said yes to God, thousands had come to know Him. LOVE COSTS! After that meeting I was so encouraged in my faith.

This Friday your dad is leaving with five other men to go to a very dangerous part of Africa to encourage 165 pastors to go forward in their faith. A place where just six months ago, 7 pastors were killed and tortured for their faith. LOVE COSTS!

Kids you may not think you are facing death, but the reality is: we all are. So either we live or die. My prayer today is that we live with love.

Love,

Mom

"Love Covers"

Good Morning Children,

Reading 1 Peter 4:7-8 we are told, *"The end of all things is near. Therefore be alert and of sober mind so that you may pray. Above all, love each other deeply, because love covers over a multitude of sins."* Paul is talking to us about relationships that exist within the church. I was thinking about how love covers a multitude of sins.

Sin is not something we ignore, avoid, or brush off, especially if it comes to us in abundance. In order for love to cover sin you must first acknowledge sin is there. Acknowledging is not announcing. It confronts and deals privately with those who have sinned against you (Matthew 18:15). This is not always an easy process and I think that is why he is teaching us to be clear minded and yet respond in self-control so that we can effectively pray and receive help from the Father to know how to respond in His love.

The passage goes on to say this happens so that we can administer God's grace in its various forms. The goal is not to destroy when we are faced with the sinfulness of others, or even when we are faced with our own sinfulness. That is the enemy's territory. The goal is to bring unity back to the body of our Lord so that His name would be glorified. His love is redemptive, not destructive. James 5:20 says, *"Whoever turns a sinner from the error of their way will save them from death and cover over a multitude of sins."* After you have worked through the difficulties and separation that sin brings, there comes a time when you take a sheet and lay it across the sin, tightly tucking in all four corners so that it doesn't give way to bitterness. God gives us the power to do this through His amazing grace and love.

I share with you today because I have been in the church long enough to know it devours its own with hatred and revenge. People who hold the sins of others in front of a mirror and never see their own reflection, publicly showing and uncovering the faults of others. I do not want that for you. I don't want that for me. I want us to be a reflection of the love of God in anything we face in life because the time is near, Kids, and at His coming the key characteristic of our life is not measured by how much we have done, or what we have learned, or if we have great faith and give all we have to the poor. Our life will be measured by how we have loved.

2 John 1:6 instructs us, *"As you have heard from the beginning, his command is that you walk in love."*

Mom

"Perfect Love Drives Out Fear"

Good Morning Children,

Rebecca St. James has a song that says, *"Until you find something worth dying for you're not really living"*. Each day is a joy because it has its plans and purposes. God has lots of plans for our life. Even if my life should end today, I believe it wouldn't stop growing in love. I try to plant seeds in other's lives that will grow into good fruit. My passion in life is to share God's love through serving and making others feel good about who they are. Death does not have its hold on me; I don't fear it. His word to me is worth dying for and each day I find less and less importance in my life, therefore, I have begun to live life to its fullness.

To me life is not worth living if God is not the center of it. How could I love? How could I forgive? How could I be a mom or wife if God's word hadn't trained me? His Word has been a model to me of life. How could I face the fears of life if I did not trust in Him? I have placed your lives in His hands. I do not know what tomorrow may hold for any of us, but I know God can see us through anything. God is my anchor in life; He holds me steady when I am in the midst of storms. Spend time with God and read His word. It is full of golden nuggets waiting to be discovered. It is your road map through life.

God's word sets you free from fears. He helps us do life the right way!

"There is no fear in love. But perfect love drives out fear, because fear has to do with punishment. The one who fears is not made perfect in love." 1 John 4:18

I love you,

Mom

"Hope"

Good Morning Children,

Grandpa Ehrgott went to be with the Lord today, October 11, 2004. Your father and I were there when he took his last breath. It was shocking, sad and at the same time peaceful. He needed to go home to be with the Lord. His body was so weak. The last week was hard for me watching him waste away. The time I spent with him before he died was precious to me. He did not complain, and his spirit was very beautiful. I saw it in the way he would hold my hand and look into my eyes, which radiated nothing but love. The way he said, *"I love you,"* or *"Thank you for being with me."* I will miss him. He was always helpful and I enjoyed seeing him. I will miss the crazy way he said hello to me when he saw me. I will treasure in my heart all the wonderful memories we shared together. You know I do not have one bad memory of him.

I was reading in 1 Thessalonians 4:13-14, *"Brothers and sisters, we do not want you to be uninformed about those who sleep in death, so that you do not grieve like the rest of mankind, who have no hope. For we believe that Jesus died and rose again, and so we believe that God will bring with Jesus those who have fallen asleep in him."*

Thank God that through Jesus we have hope! Grandpa knew and believed in Jesus as his Savior. Today He is with Him! Always place your trust in Him.

I love you,

Mom

"To Live or Die"

Good Morning Children,

Philippians 1:19-26

Some people believe that if you accept Christ all will be fine. No problems, no fears...etc. In verse 19, Paul is saying that because of your prayers and the help given through the Spirit of Jesus, what has happened to me will turn out for my deliverance. He is expecting and hoping that he would not be ashamed. I am sure during this time he remembered the words of the Lord. *"In this life you will have trouble. But take heart! I have overcome the world"* (John 16:33). *"Blessed are those who are persecuted because of righteousness, for theirs is the kingdom of heaven"* (Matthew 5:10). I am sure Paul remembered his calling recorded in Acts 9:15-16, *"This man is my chosen instrument to proclaim my name to the Gentiles and their kings and to the people of Israel. I will show him how much he must suffer for my name."*

We may not be suffering to the point of actual death, but maybe we are suffering in the relationships we have in our lives. Relationships often go wrong because we want to be in control. When we lose our right to be right...we die. Yet we live. We are confident in whom we believe in, for who we are, Kids, is determined by whom and what we place our trust in. Paul's faith was rooted in Christ. In verse 20, he prayed he would have sufficient courage because at times it is hard to stand in the face of struggles and trials. But the purpose was found in the famous quote in verse 21 of Philippians 1, *"For to me, to live is Christ and to die is gain."* The world teaches us another way, *"To live is gain, but to die is less"*. Not so Kids. Don't believe this lie. In verses 23-26, in the face of death, he chooses to live, but for one reason. To continue helping others to know of Christ's great love for them. His desire was for joy, the kind that overflows no matter what life may bring.

You may be facing different kinds of struggles today. Paul knew because of others prayers and support what was happening to him would turn out for good. I encourage you today to find those people in your life who are filled with faith to encourage you and pray for you.

I want you to know that each day Dad and I pray together for all of you.

Love,

Mom

"Attitude: Live or Die"

Good Morning Children,

Philippians 2:5-11

Our attitude has a lot to say about who we are and what we do. How do we react when we are attacked, humiliated, intimidated, or made fun of? Most would say they become defensive, revengeful, lash out or curse. Our inner self does not want to give up or give in. It does not want to die or be threatened in anyway. It strives to be alive and in control. It wants to win in everything. The questions it keeps asking are: How can I get what I want? How soon can I get it? What do I have to pay to get it? It tells us success is measured by my achievements and the position I hold.

Paul wants to teach us another way. He says in verse 5 that our attitude should be the same as Christ. So what is that? Jesus addressed this problem himself in Mark 10:35-45.

James and John wanted to be number one. They sought position and standing. Listen to their request to Jesus. *"'Teacher', they said, 'we want you to do for us whatever we ask.' 'What do you want me to do for you?' They replied, 'Let one of us sit at your right and the other at your left in your glory.'"* They wanted to be first and have glory and have the seat of importance. I love what Jesus did. He did not rebuke them but asked them a question. *"Can you drink the cup I drink...?"* Yea, we can! Ok, then Jesus says, *"...whoever wants to become great among you must be your servant, and whoever wants to be first must be slave of all. For even the Son of Man did not come to be served, but to serve..."*

In verses 6 and 7, Paul lets us know that Christ who being in the very nature God, made himself nothing. He gave up His rights, He emptied himself, taking on the very nature of a servant. He humbled himself and became obedient to the point of death. But in doing so, verses 9-11 show us He was exalted to the highest place, was given a name above every name, a name that every knee will bow and confess that He is Lord, to the glory of the Father.

A man asked a Rabbi: *"How come in the olden days God would show Himself to the people, but today nobody ever sees God? The Rabbi said, "Because nowadays, nobody can bow low enough."*

Father, help us to go low enough to see clearly who you are.

Love you all,

Mom

"The Christian Life is a Shared Life"

Good Morning Children,

Philippians 2:1-4

Mother Teresa said she found that loneliness is one of the worst poverty's there is. The rich and the poor share in its sorrows. I would venture to say a lot of Christians are lonely. It doesn't mean they don't have friends. Some have lots of friends, but they are not sharing their life. Most friendships are surface and not deep. Along the way we have been hurt and it makes us not want to share anything with anyone. Paul addresses this issue:

Verse 1
IF you have any encouragement from being united with Christ
IF any comfort from his love
IF any fellowship with the Spirit
IF any tenderness
IF any compassion

Verse 2
THEN make my joy complete:
(Ways to have great friendships)
1. By being like-minded (interests)
2. By having the same kind of love (Christian fellowship)
3. By being one in the Spirit (unity)
4. By being one in purpose (going in the same direction)

Verse 3

(Ways not to have great friends)

1. By having selfish ambition. (Don't use your friends to gain anything that would promote you.)

2. By being conceited. (Don't exalt yourself or think of yourself better than your friend.)

Paul is saying in verses 3-4, if you want true fellowship, then humble yourself and consider your friends better than yourself. And while you are taking care of and providing for yourself, be sure to also look out for the interest of others. To do this, Kids, is to bridge the gap. It shows we truly care for each other. Abraham Maslow, one of the giant thinkers of the twentieth century, did a study on human behavior. He ended it by saying, "*Without exception, I found that every person who was sincerely happy, radiantly alive, was living for a purpose or a cause beyond himself.*"

Live beyond yourself Kids.

I love you,

Mom

"Obey"

Good Morning Children,

Philippians 2:12-13

Can you ever remember telling me you were going to do something and you didn't? In my presence you had an intention to obey, but once I was out of sight and out of mind you did whatever you wanted?

Paul had this to say about the Philippians in verse 12, "...*you have always obeyed - not only in my presence, but now much more in my absence...*" I was thinking today about how I might work out my salvation more if I kept in mind that God was seeing everything I do. I am sure I would tremble or fear at my actions because the fact is I don't obey as I should at times.

Verse 13 says, "...*for it is God who works in you to will and to act in order to fulfill his good purpose.*" I am thankful it is God who works in me. It is because of His love and purpose in my life that drives me to do what is right.

I started thinking, why do we work out? To develop, to grow, to produce, to build up, to mature, to feel better, and to look better. The same is true with the workout we do to produce growth spiritually in us. We have to work out each day. It has to do with trust, obedience, endurance, and assurance that God has a plan for our lives, one that is not based on our will, but on His.

To obey or disobey? The choice is ours.

Love you,

Mom

"Puppets and Plans"

Good Morning Children,

As I share with others my experiences, people want to know why God does not take care of the children who are poor. They say, *"If there is a God, He wouldn't let the people starve,"* or *"Why does He cause people to do terrible things?"* I was asked these questions three times Saturday. The following was my answer:

Puppets

God did not make us like puppets. He doesn't cause sin. He gave us free will and hopefully one that would choose to serve Him, not because we have to, but because we want to. For what is love if we are made to love? I told those who had asked that I have four children. Making them love me would not give me pleasure, but if they chose to love me it would fill me with joy. I believe God is the same way with His children. He gave us a choice to love Him. It gives Him great joy to see His children walking in love, and as we love others, we are loving Him back.

The Plan

God gave us the plan. It was His only Son and He sent Him to us in the flesh. Jesus taught us how to love, give, and share, so that no one would be in need. He spent His life with the poor. He chose to live among them. The problem is not with God doing His job, it is with us. We do not get the plan. The truth is there are people starving, drinking dirty water, and children left unprotected. Why? It isn't because God did not care. It is because we didn't. I am sure His heart breaks for His children.

I also believe He is looking for someone to go for Him. To be his feet, his hands, and arms. To give out of the blessings He has given to us.

The choice is still ours.

Isaiah 6:8 says, *"Then I heard the voice of the Lord saying, 'Whom shall I send? And who will go for us?' And I said, 'Here am I. Send me!'"*

Kids, we are not a puppet waiting for God to pick us up. He has already given us hands to serve, arms to hold, eyes to see, talents to share, money to give…etc.

Today someone is waiting on you. Is it God?

I love you,

Mom

"Peace"

Good Morning Children,

We have been studying Colossians in our Bible Study. I really enjoyed this last week. We are on chapter 3 verse 15, *"Let the peace of God rule in your hearts...* What does it mean *"let"*? *"To give opportunity to or fail to prevent"* is how www.merriam-webster.com defines it. I thought about a door and allowing or letting someone in, and then I asked myself, *"Do I allow or let God's peace in my life? Do I receive it as a gift?"*

Jesus said in John 14:27, *"Peace I leave you; my peace I give you. I do not give to you as the world gives. Do not let your hearts be troubled and do not be afraid."* I would say if I am worrying, I do not have peace. Yet peace does not mean that there is not going to be conflict in my life, but rather in that conflict or set of circumstances I am able to still find peace. Like Paul in prison...singing. God was his source of peace, not circumstances.

So, how do I do this? By focusing on God instead of what my circumstances are and to let Christ rule in my heart. What does it mean to rule? That definition is that as an umpire calls the shots in a game, so God should be calling the shots in our lives.

I also asked myself what causes me to lose my peace? Here are some things I listed.

1. When I do not feel I measure up...I'm not good enough
2. When I have sin in my life
3. When I begin to control things

4. When I do not stay in the word or fellowship
5. When I have conflict in a relationship

I don't know what your list is, but I do know Christ is the Prince of Peace.

Hope you all have a day filled with the peace of God. LET Him rule in your HEARTS.

Love,

Mom

"Fasting"

Good Morning Children,

I was reading Isaiah 58 this morning. It is about fasting. It is something we all should be doing. But what is it? Verse 1 through 5 talks about what it is not. Day after day people sought God out, but with wrong motives. Verse 2 states, *"...they SEEM eager to know my ways, as if they were a nation that does what is right..."* In verse 3 they question God asking, *"'Why have we fasted,' they say, 'and you have not seen it? Why have we humbled ourselves, and you have not noticed?'"* They just wanted to appear to be religious and to magnify their own performance. Continuing in verse 3 through the end of verse 5, the Lord responded to them, *"Yet on the day of your fasting, you do as you please and exploit all your workers. Your fasting ends in quarreling and strife, and in striking each other with wicked fists. You cannot fast as you do today and expect your voice to be heard on high. Is this the kind of fast I have chosen, only a day for people to humble themselves? Is it only for bowing one's head like a reed and for lying in sackcloth and ashes? Is that what you call a fast, a day acceptable to the Lord?"*

Then the scripture tells us in verse 6 of the true fast that is pleasing to the Lord.

1. To lose the chains of injustice
2. To set the oppressed people free
3. To share your food with the hungry
4. To provide the poor with shelter
5. To clothe the naked

Kids, fasting is a matter of the heart. We never want to appear to be religious on the outside and be filled with hatred on the inside. There are times we set aside to seek the Lord, but seeking is active and gives direction in practical ways. We also should be seeking His will and not our own. I love the result or promise of seeking the Lord with all our heart that we see starting in verse 8.

1. Light will break forth like the dawn.
2. Healing will quickly appear.
3. Righteousness will go before you.
4. The Glory of the Lord will follow you.
5. I love this one, *"Then you will call, and the Lord will answer; you will cry for help, and he will say: Here I am."*
6. If you spend yourself in behalf of the hungry, satisfy the needs of the oppressed. Then *"light will rise in the darkness, and your night will become like the noonday."*
7. The Lord will guide you, satisfy your needs, and strengthen your frame.
8. You will be like a well-watered garden, a spring whose waters never fail.
9. You will be called the repairer of broken walls, restorer of streets with dwelling…wow!

"A matter of the heart", Kids. I pray today as we seek the Lord, our hearts would melt in his presence. How awesome is His love…

Love you all,

Mom

"*Gossip*"

Good Morning Children,

Oh no, not this one! Ears perk up and I seem to give attention to it. It's the bait the enemy hangs out in front of us. We want to know more. It's powerful and deadly. Beware and be alert. It seeks anyone and pulls them into a tangled web never to undo. It hurts, destroys and betrays. It's very well disguised and uses truth as an excuse. Who am I? What is it? Its name is Gossip.

Every one of us have spoken the fruit of this deadly sin. Many have lost friends or broken the heart of someone. Oh, it is all done in the name of *"I'm telling you this so you can pray."* or *"Promise not to tell?"* or *"Don't tell anyone, but did you know."* or even, *"Know what I heard?"*

Gossip, what is it anyway? It is a person who habitually spreads intimate or private rumors or facts about another ones confidence or business. What do the scriptures say about gossiping? *"A gossip betrays a confidence; so avoid anyone who talks too much"* (Proverbs 20:19). *"A perverse person stirs up conflict, and a gossip separates close friends"* (Proverbs 16:28).

What if the next time we heard, *"I'm not supposed to tell…"* we said, *"Then don't! I don't want to know."* I think even if we are not the one telling we are just as guilty if we eat of the fruit of gossip. It tempts us to tell someone else and before you know it, a lot of people have heard. And someone will get hurt.

Holy Spirit, I ask today you would convict our hearts whenever we speak or give ear to gossip. Forgive us, and give us a discerning heart when we speak about others. Amen.

Have a great day,

Mom

"The King"

Good Morning Children,

When I was a kid we played *"King of the Mountain"*. A person would get on top of the mountain and try to protect his or her position. Knees bent, gritting their teeth, arms extended, ready to fight anyone who tried to take over. *"King! King!"* we would yell from the top of the hill. *"I rule!"* Guy's would beat their chest as if they were King Kong.

Power. People love it and most would do anything for it, even if it's just for a moment. 1 Timothy 6:15 says this, *"...God will bring about in his own time – God, the blessed and only Ruler, the King of kings and Lord of lords"*. He did not rule on top of the mountain, but as a humble servant below.

Perhaps today you may be the one who is on top of the mountain, just waiting for someone to dare try to move you. It's your position. You got there all by yourself, and you'll fight to the end.

So my thought is this: Never climb a mountain where you are the only one standing.

Love,

Mom

"*Power*"

Good Morning Children,

Last week at Bible Study, someone was giving a presentation on power. She told us a quote she was using from Abe Lincoln. "*Nearly all men can stand adversity, but if you want to test a man's character give him power.*" I thought of this all week. I started thinking about David's life and how power changed him from a shepherd boy to a king. In the story of David and Bathsheba, David used other people in his influence to bring a married woman to himself. He raped this woman and got her pregnant. He tried to put the blame on someone else. He ends up ordering her husband to be killed. The story can be found in 2 Samuel 11.

The scriptures say God was displeased with David and He sent Nathan to confront David. In chapter 12 starting in verse 7 the Lord says to David, "*I anointed you king over Israel* (God gave him position), *and I delivered you from the hand of Saul.* (God gave him protection*) I gave your master's house to you and your master's wives into your arms.* (God gave him provision) *I gave you all Israel and Judah.*" (God gave him power)

Romans 12:3 says, "*For by the grace given me I say to every one of you: Do not think of yourself more highly than you ought, but rather think of yourself with sober judgment, in accordance with the faith God has distributed to each of you.*" In other words God is the one who gives us all things, when we think we have earned it on our own is when we begin to build pride in our self. It says I can do whatever I want. I have earned the right. It all depends on me. I can make it happen. We begin to rely on our self instead of God who is the giver of all things.

The best way to be a leader is to be an example. To love and respect others the way you want to be treated. When you use your position as power and you begin to manipulate people, know that this is a trap the devil uses to manipulate you. In the end it leads to destruction. David's sin cost him a lot, but when confronted, he confessed. All of us fall short in so many areas, but when the light of God's word shines in our hearts may it cause us to fall on our face and confess only God has the power. He gives it to those who use it for His Glory.

To God be the Glory forever and ever. Amen.

I love you,

Mom

"*Pride*"

Good Morning Children,

Who is the most powerful person you know? I was reading this morning about the story of King Uzziah in 2 Chronicles 26. He was a powerful king and as long as he sought the Lord, God gave him success. He went to war and God helped him. His fame spread and he became a very powerful King. He surrounded himself with royal families, well trained armies, officers and a lot of trained, skilled men. But his fame and power became his downfall. Verses 15 and 16 tell us, *"His fame spread far and wide, for he was greatly helped until he became powerful. But after Uzziah became powerful, his pride led to his downfall. He was unfaithful to the Lord his God..."*

In this story I found some keys that can help test us to see if we have allowed pride or the misuse of power to enter into our lives.

1. Pride always says, *"I am better than the laws. The rules don't apply to me. I allow others to overlook my offensives. I am accountable to no one."* The King did something that was forbidden to do.
2. When I am confronted, do I become angry and try to defend myself? The King became angry and enraged, and says, *"How dare you tell me what to do."*
3. Am I critical, puffed up? The King lashed out at the priests. After all he thought, if I can use my power to belittle and tear down, I will get my way.
4. Pride does not yield when confronted. It defends its rights, even when it knows it's wrong.

5.   Pride does not rejoice in the position of others. The priest had rights and positions to be where they were and to do what was required of them. The King saw only his agenda and his wants. Pride cannot rejoice when others succeed.

So Kids, how can we protect ourselves from pride? In verse 5, *"As long as he sought the Lord, God gave him success."* I think the key is knowing who is King and submitting ourselves to God who is our King. We never should use our positions to exalt ourselves or allow others to let us live above the laws. Proverbs 18:12, *"Before a downfall the heart is haughty, but humility comes before honor."* Your mother's wisdom for the day is this: *"Instead of surrounding yourself with those that can help you or make you look good. Surround yourself with those you can help and make them look better."*

I love you,

Mom

"The Winds of Life"

Good Morning Children,

In the story of Peter walking on water, the disciples were all in the boat in the midst of the storm. It does not say they were afraid of the wind, after all they were fishermen and I am sure they had been in plenty of storms. But something happened that was different. Jesus came to them walking on the water. They were terrified! He said to them, *"Do not be afraid."*

Peter wanted to come to Jesus. *"Come,"* Jesus replied. Peter got out of the boat and began to walk on the water, but when he saw the wind he became afraid and began to sink. *"Lord, save me,"* Peter said. Immediately Jesus reached out His hand and caught him. *"You of little faith, why did you doubt?"* (Matthew 14:22-31).

I have been meditating on this passage for a couple of days. Here are my thoughts and questions. When he saw the winds, hadn't he noticed them before? Who really see's the wind? We see the effects of the wind and the damage it can do, but who makes the wind blow? Where does it come from and why? Sometimes we are tossed about by the winds of life. Most of the time we don't understand them, yet we can be tormented by them. Peter was obviously out of his comfort zone and understanding. Things just didn't make sense. That is when he saw or noticed the wind. He knew its power. He became powerless. He was out of control.

Kid's, I pray all is well in your lives, but I can guarantee you that there will come a time that you will become powerless. Everything around you becomes different and you may not understand why. It may be your job, a relationship, a death. All hell has been released and you will feel like you are about to drown. What will you do? This story has the answer...

"Come," Jesus says when Peter began to sink. Jesus' hand was just a reach away. He is always there ready to catch us in times of trouble. All we need to do is ask for His help. When I come to the place when I am so comfortable in life and I don't acknowledge who blows the wind, I realize that I have become self-sufficient and arrogant doing what I know how to do without acknowledging any help from God. It is in these times God has a way of getting my attention. He will come to me in ways He never has before. He has a way of getting my focus back inline so I can see He is the author of everything I am and do because without Him I am nothing. His words are as important as the air I breathe. Please read them every day. Thank Him for all He does and better yet for who He is. For without Him I don't know where I would be or even who I would be. To God be all the glory and may we never fail to see Him in new ways.

I love you all,

Mom

"Persistence, Justice and Faith"

Good Morning Children,

Jesus told a story of a persistent widow to teach us that we should always pray and not give up. In the story, a widow comes to a judge asking and pleading for him to grant her justice from her oppressor. He refused for quite some time. This man neither feared God nor had any concern for men, but because she kept coming and bothering him he saw to it that she got justice. Then, the Lord says, *"Listen to what the unjust judge says. And will not God bring about justice for his chosen ones, who cry out to him day and night? Will he keep putting them off?"* But this story ends with this phrase, *"...when the Son of Man comes, will he find faith on the earth?"* (Luke 18:1-8).

As I thought about this story, I was intrigued by the fact that this widow asked for justice to be granted. Often times, people are screaming for their rights to be justified. We come to God and tell him how to answer and when, and then what we want done. Over and over again we knock, yell, and scream at others to defend our rights. We make judgments based on how we feel without even asking God His. *"Will God find faith on the earth?"* I look at this widow's prayer and it says to me she was leaving it in the hands of the judge saying, *"Please grant me justice. You make the call. Hand down the verdict. I trust you."*

Kid's, that is faith here on earth. When you feel alone, desperate, violated, or misrepresented go to God, night and day, and ask God for His justice to be served. Be persistent. When we allow God to take our case it frees us from bitterness, hatred or even murderous thoughts. In the end, Kid's, we will all take our stand in front of Him.

"And the heavens proclaim his righteousness, for he is a God of justice" (Psalm 50:6).

Lord, thank you for hearing us and that you are a God who cares about the concerns of men. Thank you that you are the Just Judge. Lord, teach us to pray for those who have hurt us or spoken evil against us. Help us to honor those on earth you have put in control of the courts. May you give them a genuine concern for the people they serve. Grant us faith. Thank you for loving us and caring for us. To Him alone be the Glory.

I love you,

Mom

"Rejoice"

Good Morning Children,

"The Lord has done it this very day; let us rejoice today and be glad" (Psalm 118:24).

Today may be one of those days that you wonder, *"What is there to rejoice about?"* You may be going through all kinds of emotions and situations, but have you ever stopped to think and then you realized all of it is good? God gave us all kinds of emotions. Love, joy, anger, hurt… etc. Instead of reacting or acting out on them why don't we ask God about them? *"Lord, I am hurting today. What happened? Please help me."* I am learning that whenever I am in need or offended by something that most of the time it is something that is within me that God wants to work on. *"Search me, God, and know my heart; test me and know my anxious thoughts. See if there is any offensive way in me, and lead me in the way everlasting"* (Psalm 139:23-24).

Don't look past your own heart Kids. Fault finding begins with you first. There is only one God, and sadly enough, it is not us. God will always lead us with a thankful heart even when it is offended. We have so much to be thankful for like another day we get to work on becoming more like Him. Yikes! It's going to be a busy day! Love you all so much!

Rejoice,

Mom

"Open Doors"

Good Morning Children,

I had an interesting phone call this week. It was from the jail. Someone had requested I come to see them. When I asked who it was, I was shocked. It was from a girl I had helped a lot! This girl had used and abused our relationship until it was no more. So, why was she calling me?

Last year I went through training at the jail to be able to work with inmates. I did this because I wanted to let them know their life was valuable to God and that He has a plan for them. Had anything changed?

When I got the call I was shocked, but I was filled with compassion. I am sure she had no one. I was glad I got the call because somehow in our relationship I had left an open door, one she knew she could walk through. Sometimes we walk through life shutting doors and bolting them shut. Even if God were to knock would we open the door?

Romans 15:1-4 teaches us that we ought to bear the failings of others, and not just do things that would be pleasing to us, but pleasing to others, to build them up. Christ took upon Himself the insults of others to teach us that through endurance and the encouragement of the scriptures we might have hope. My friend needs hope.

My prayer for you and me today is in verses 5 and 6. *"May the God who gives endurance and encouragement give you the same attitude of mind toward each other that Christ Jesus had, so that with one mind and one voice you may glorify the God and Father of our Lord Jesus Christ."*

I love you,

Mom

P.S. My door is always open.

"*Live*"

Good Morning Children,

"How do you want me to live my life Lord?" This is a question I seem to keep asking in many different ways. *"What is pleasing to you? What is your will for my life? How can I make your name known to the world?"* This morning I was reading Ephesians 5:1, *"Follow God's example, therefore, as dearly loved children and walk in the way of love, just as Christ loved us and gave himself up for us as a fragrant offering and sacrifice to God."*

The goal, Kids, is to represent Christ in the earth so others may come to know Him. Not in what we say or even how much we know, but how we live our lives out each day. How we treat one another. People are watching and making judgments on how we live only to see if it matches up with what we say. Sometimes it is hard to live a life of love. It helped me this morning to know that even Christ's love was a sacrifice offered to God. Christ gave Himself up. Do I give myself and my agenda's up? I don't feel like loving at times, but if I can look at it as a way to please God by offering and sacrificing my own feelings, it will be pleasing and acceptable to Him.

Everyone has a need to be loved. In this passage I smile because I know I am dearly loved. We have been given a gift today. The gift of life. We have been given the opportunity to give it away as Christ did for us. Someone today needs a smile.

Live a life of love,

Mom

P.S. I dearly love you all.

"Live: A Life of Love"

Good Morning Children,

1 John 4:16-17 states, *"God is love. Whoever lives in love lives in God, and God in them. This is how love is made complete among us so that we will have confidence on the day of judgment: In this world we are like Jesus."*

Kids, how do we have confidence on the Day of Judgment when we stand before God? Did you know that your life right now is on trial? Well, it is. How we live our lives today will determine where we live tomorrow.

So you can know with confidence, let's enter the courtroom. God is on the throne and I am standing before Him. The evidence has been recorded. He can say to me, *"[Sandy], I was hungry and you gave me something to eat. I was thirsty and you gave me something to drink. I was a stranger and you invited me in. I needed clothes and you clothed me. I was sick and you looked after me. I was in prison and you came to see me."* Then I will say, *"When Lord did I do this?"* *"Whenever you did it for the least of my children you did it to me."* Or He could say to me, *"[Sandy], when I was hungry, thirsty, a stranger, in need of clothes, sick or in prison, you did nothing to look after me"* (Matthew 25:31-46).

So then the judgment is made on how I lived my life in love for others, but what is the verdict? Guilty or innocent? What is my sentence?

If I have lived my life in love to others he says to me, *"Come, take your inheritance, the kingdom prepared for you since the creation of the world."* But if I have not lived a life of love towards others, He will say to me,

"Go away to eternal punishment." We say we love God, but the truth is found in the way we love others.

Kids, Jesus loves his family just like we do. He died for them, he spent a lifetime teaching us how to love, give, and serve. I know it breaks His heart that His children are hungry, thirsty, sick, naked and imprisoned. How will we love Him today?

I love you and I pray I love others in the same way.

Mom

"*Live*"

"We live by faith, not by sight." 2 Corinthians 5:7

Good Morning Children,

Often we live by sight, and not by faith. We want all the details. We want to see before we get something. To me living by faith is a huge trust issue. Do we really trust God knows what is best? Will He take care of us?

So what is faith? Hebrews 11:1, *"Now faith is confidence in what we hope for and assurance about what we do not see."* Hebrews 11:6 says, *"And without faith it is impossible to please God, because anyone who comes to him must believe that he exists and that he rewards those who earnestly seek him."* Living by faith is where we offer our lives to God and trust Him to see for us.

WHAT? Surrender control of my life? Are you crazy?! Yep! That's what I'm talking about. Crazy in love with a God that sees the future. One who loves me and cares about my life more than anyone else ever will. A God who has the best plans and benefits for me.

Live by faith? Is it easy? No! Most of the time our prayer is, *"God, show me the way."* Jesus replies, *"My sheep know my voice. You know the way."* *"But…just give me a sign,"* we beg. His reply was, *"Nope."* You see it goes back to trust. Showing is too easy, it does not require faith.

Kids, all I can say is living by faith gets easier the more you practice it. To live by faith is a great adventure. You never know what is ahead, but the more you trust the more you begin to really live.

Desire what you cannot see.

Mom

"*Live*"

"Be very careful, then, how you live…" Ephesians 5:15

"Good Morning Children,"

We have a warning today, from this passage, to live a life of wisdom and to make the most of every opportunity. (Ephesians 5:16) What opportunities has life presented to you lately? How have you reacted? Paul gives us some great insight. He tells us not to be foolish or in other words, don't just react, but actually understand what the Lord's will is. He goes on to say not to be drunk, but to *be filled with the Spirit, speaking to one another with psalms, hymns, and songs from the Spirit. Sing and make music from your heart to the Lord, always giving thanks to God…"* (Eph. 5:17-20).

Sometimes we don't know what to do in life. That is why it is so important to read God's word to gain wisdom, to surround ourselves with Christian friends for encouragement, and to be thankful in everything so we can fight off bitterness.

As I think about being careful how I live, I have to ask the question, *"Who is in control of my life? Do I live to please myself or do I live to please the Lord?"* Opportunity awaits for you today. Live.

I love you,

Mom

"Live: For Who Do We Live?"

Good Morning Children,

1 Corinthians 8:6 says, *"…there is but one Lord, Jesus Christ, through whom all things came and for whom we live; and there is but one Lord, Jesus Christ, through whom all things came and through whom we live."*

If Christ is whom I live for, then what does that mean? Maybe that is not about me. Maybe I live for my plans and agendas. Often times we live for what we want, or like. But what does God want? What does He like? Does that match up with what I want? How would our lives change if daily we recognized who we live for? Acts 17:28 says, *"For in him we live and move and have our being."* Today you will have plenty of opportunities and choices. The question is…For whom will you live?

I love you,

Mom

"Live: Live as Children of the Light"

Ephesians 5:8-21

Good Morning Children,

In Matthew 5 Jesus said, *"You are the light of the world"* (Verse 14). *"…let your light shine before others, that they may see your good deeds and glorify your Father in heaven"* (Verse 16). You may think your light is not very bright right now, but think with me for a minute. You are in a dark cave, no light at all. You strike a small match and it lights up the whole room. Light, no matter how bright, dispels darkness. Even if you just have a spark, God can ignite it.

Ephesians 5:9-14 tells us, *"…the fruit of this light consists in all goodness, righteousness and truth) and find out what pleases the Lord. Have nothing to do with the fruitless deeds of darkness, but rather expose them. It is shameful even to mention what the disobedient do in secret. But everything exposed by the light becomes visible-and everything that is illuminated becomes a light."* You see it is light that makes everything visible. This is why it continues to say, *"Wake up, sleeper, rise from the dead, and Christ will shine on you"* (Eph. 5:14).

Remember the little song we used to sing, *"This Little Light of Mine"*? It goes like this…*This little light of mine, I'm gonna let it shine…Hide it under a bushel, NO! I'm gonna let it shine…Don't let Satan blow it out. I'm gonna let it shine. Let it shine, let it shine, let it shine.* Shine!

Love you,

Mom

"Hope Lives"

Good Morning Children,

Several years ago, I visited a village of squatters that live near the abandoned airport in Nicaragua. The people who lived there were very poor. I recall meeting two little boys who couldn't have been more dirty and covered with sores. The clothes they wore were rags. They lived in a house that was no more than wrapped plastic. I had the opportunity to meet their mother. She was just as dirty as they were and covered with the same bites up and down her arms. They had no running water. While talking to her, I asked her what her greatest need was at the moment. With tears in her eyes she told me that she wanted her children to go to school, but she needed to get birth certificates and a sponsor to help send them. I never forgot them and had taken a photo of them to bring back home in hopes of getting them some help. I talked to my friend, Karen, about the possibility of becoming involved in their lives. She said she believed it was a good time for her because she had just finished supporting another child through school and wanted to do it again.

She began to help and I would visit them each time I went back to Nicaragua. I would give letters and pictures that my friend sent with me to the woman. They began to look different each time I saw them. I saw smiles instead of tears. Hope had filled their lives.

Then two years ago, my friend went with me to Nicaragua. I will never forget it. As ten women got out of the van, the little boy she supports ran up to her and said, "I knew it was you!" She had the opportunity to meet the family she had been investing in face to face. They came to where we were staying and visited with her. When we got home she said, *"I want to buy them chickens so they will always have food."* When I went back I gave the money to the pastor and they got chickens.

In December of last year, my sister and granddaughter went with me to see them. Chickens were everywhere! When I asked the boy what he wanted for Christmas he said, *"Karen."* Karen returned with me in September, and it was a great reunion. She got to spend a lot of time with them including taking them to a food court and a movie, which was the first time ever to do something like that. Karen spent several hours talking with the mom. I remember walking past them and Karen, who is a nurse, was rubbing an ointment on her arms. At least I thought that was what I saw. What I actually saw was love; Jesus reaching out through the hands of my friend. I tell you all this because of what love does to a family when we share what we have been given to those who don't have. What happens is HOPE. Many of you know of the same joys I am talking about as you have become involved in the lives of those you support. I would just like to say thank you for giving, for loving and bringing HOPE.

"May the God of hope fill you with all joy and peace as you trust in him, so that you may overflow with hope by the power of the Holy Spirit" (Romans 15:13).

Love you all,

Mom

"God Chose Me"

Good Morning Children,

The vast difference between two worlds is constantly before me as never before. It is as if I am walking around either crying or smiling. Both worlds tug at my heart and I wonder who I am again or have I forgotten why God choose me to begin with.

My reading this morning was 1 Corinthians 1:26-29, *"Brothers and sisters, think of what you were when you were called. Not many of you were wise by human standards; not many were influential; not many were of noble birth. But God chose the foolish things of the world to shame the wise; God chose the weak things of the world to shame the strong. God chose the lowly things of this world and the despised things – and the things that are not – to nullify the things that are, so that no one may boast before him."*

In conclusion, to my reading I thought, *"God chose those who have nothing to brag about and are not impressive."* The first part of this verse says to think of what you were when you were called. Kids, I was a nobody, or at least I felt that way. I was not educated or influential, nor was I born into noble family. Yet, God chose me. Perhaps somewhere along the way I have begun to think I am a person of influence or that I have become wise or impressive. Or that perhaps God in some way needs me. But God doesn't need me, He chose me. All that I am is because of Him. I know I must decrease and He must increase more and more in my life. Perhaps this is what the children were teaching me. Whenever I am with them I see the face of God, His Glory! Those who have nothing, but yet have everything. In the next few weeks I'll share with you my journey there. I am so thankful for each of you and I give God glory!

I love you all,

Mom

"Giving Without Questioning"

Good Morning Children,

We were in a church service our second day in Africa and as I was worshipping God I heard, *"Give your Bible to the lady next to you." "What?! My Bible? My mission Bible? The one I have taught from, underlined, and had all my notes in…the one that holds my thoughts and all the things you have taught me over the years?"* I quickly started worshipping God again, but as soon as I did I heard it again, *"Give the lady your Bible."* To be honest I was a little nervous. The thought came to my mind that we had brought Bibles to give away, so I said to the Lord, *"God, I know one of my gifts is giving, but perhaps this is just me thinking and not really you. But if you really want her to have my Bible then I really need to know it is you. So if it is you, have her ask me for my Bible."* Kids, this lady had not spoken a word to me but as soon as I finished praying, she tapped me on the shoulder and pointed to the center of my Bible and said, *"I want this Bible."* Without hesitation I said, *"Ok, you can have it. I'll give it to you after the service."*

I have thought a lot about that situation. The questions I keep asking myself are, *"Why couldn't I just have obeyed the first time? Why did I offer Him something else that cost me nothing? Why couldn't I see God using the gift He had placed in my life? Why did I even ask Him to prove Himself to me? Why did I feel I had to hold on to it a little longer? Why do I think sometimes God wants something from me instead of thinking how much God wants to give me?"* I still have so much growing to do.

After I gave the lady my Bible, I was so excited for her and wondered if the things I had taken notes on were the very things God was going to use to bless her. My prayer for us this morning is one I am praying for me. It was Samuel's response to God's voice in 1 Samuel 3:9, *"Speak, Lord, for your servant is listening."*

I love you all,

Mom

"Genuine Love"

Good Morning Children,

In Philippians 2:19-24, Paul is speaking of Timothy and how there is no one else like him in his life. He described him as a man who had pure and genuine motives when it came to the welfare of others. Verse 21 is a key verse, *"For everyone looks out for their own interests, not those of Jesus Christ."* We define ourselves as Christians, but what does that mean? Early Christians did not call themselves Christians, others did. It was a title they were given because of the way they lived and acted. They were recognized as a group of people who followed Christ. They were Christ-like, followers of Christ, Christians. The theme of their life was loving others. They remembered one of the greatest commandments the Lord had taught them: *"Love your neighbor as yourself..."* Why? *"So that all men will know that you are my disciples."*

I have to ask myself, *"Am I known as a Christian because of the way I live my life or is it a title I have used to describe myself? Do people recognize I am different than the world? Am I Christ-like? Do I really seek the good of others? Do I treat others with respect? Do I serve in a way that would cost me something?"* The answer is, *"I WANT TO!"* I know within myself I cannot love genuinely just because I decide I want to. I must first love God with all my heart, soul and mind because it is His love in me that reaches out to others.

Kids, when we recognize how much we have already been given and how much we have been loved, we desire to share love with others. As we spend time loving God, His love just spills out as we draw close to Him. He draws close to us. He is our source of genuineness. Paul said

Timothy had proved himself in the work of the Gospel (Verse 22). There is a whole world out there today that wants proof of a living, forgiving God. So I wonder…will they see Him today?

Love,

Mom

"The Dump"

Good Morning Children,

I have been trying to process my most recent trip to Nicaragua. I grew in my understanding of poverty a little more and I am left wondering about life and how I can be more involved in my relationship with poor. What does Jesus require of us when we see our brothers and sisters suffering? Do we turn our heads in denial? I am overwhelmed with the magnitude of need. Wondering how in the world did human life get to this place.

As I sit here this morning with tears running down my face, I am overwhelmed by suffering. As I get up each day and as I go about my day, I have in my vision a scene I will never forget. I visited the dump, a place where Managua dumps its trash. I climbed up a hill and overlooked this site and as far as I could see were mountains of trash. Smoke came up from these mounds. The immense heat caused combustion; red embers of fire were in them. Men, women and children were on top digging through all of it to find food or things to recycle. I saw and spoke to little children, some were naked and all had sores on their skin. Although the sores did appear to be on the outside, it was as if the sores were coming from within. They were black with dirt and soot and the smell in the air was awful. On top of the hill I saw shacks where people lived and a lake filled with trash that had a green layer of algae on it. I saw dump trucks going through the dump, none of which seemed to stop or slow down in regards to the people. One hundred and sixty-eight families live in that dump, most never going outside its borders.

Many people have asked how my trip was. I respond, *"I visited hell."* Jesus described hell in Mark 9:48 as a place where, *"the worms that eat them do not die, and the fire is not quenched."* Kids, this was hell on earth. The fires do not go out. Worms do not die in a dump and the fire is not quenched. I asked myself, *"God, are you here??? Where are you?"* In my spirit I heard Him say, *"I AM. I AM HERE."* I saw Him in the eyes of the little children, compelling me once again to come to Him. For if I give a drink, clothe, or give to them in any way, I give to Jesus.

Kids each day we have this opportunity to give and serve our Lord. Today my prayer is that we may see Him. God's answer to a dying world, God's plan for us, is found in Isaiah 6:8, *"Then I heard the voice of the Lord saying, 'Whom shall I send? And who will go for us?' And I said, 'Here am I. Send me!'"* Go forward Kids. Jesus is waiting.

Love you all so very much,

Mom

"Follow the Way of Love"

Good Morning Children,

To follow is to imitate someone or to go after in the same direction. While in Florida, I was doing morning devotions with my granddaughters. We were reading 1 Corinthians 13 about what it means to love someone. In verse 3 it says, *"If I give all I possess to the poor and give over my body to hardship that I may boast, but do not have love, I gain nothing."* We continued to read and I began talking to them about 1 Corinthians 14:1, *"Follow the way of love..."* I shared with them about my recent trip to Africa. I told them some people think I should just send the money and not go. Both of them said, *"Nana, if you didn't go who would be there to help them? Who would hold them?"* Then I asked them this question, *"How would you like it if I only sent you money and never came to see you?"* They answered, *"We would not like that! You would not be with us and we could not hold you or go anywhere with you."*

I also asked Faith, an African Pastor, what Africans thought about Americans coming, and she said, *"It is good because whites in our country don't like us. They don't sit next to us or touch us. They look down on us. To have you come here and sit, hold, play and teach the children shows them they are important and loved."* Loving is a lifestyle we live out and follow each day. Wherever He leads me I will follow. It may be in the form of a visit, a touch, a kind word, a phone call, or a smile...all of which are free! My prayer for us today is that we would all follow the way of love, and never substitute anything for it.

Hugs and kisses,

Mom

"In My Father's House"

Good Morning Children,

One of the most popular songs the children love to sing with your dad in Africa is called *"In My Father's House"*. Some of the lyrics are:

Come and go with me
To my Father's house
Come and go with me
To my Father's house

This morning I was thinking about this song while I was reading the book of Haggai. It was all about building My Father's House. When I think about His house I think about people, the ones who fill it with His glory. Haggai is the shortest book in the Old Testament and it really made me think today. In fact five times the words *"to give careful thought to"* appear. Here are some of my thoughts after reading this book.

Chapter 1, verse 2 contains the excuses people use for not building His house. The Lord says that people say, *"The time has not yet come to rebuild the Lord's house."* I hear these exact excuses out of my own mouth. *"I will Lord…when I have the time, money… etc."* Or I say, *"I will when I get this or that done."* In verse 4 the question the Lord says is, *"Is it time for you yourselves to be living in your paneled houses, while this house remains a ruin?"* I began to think of the ruins of where I just came from. I had to ask myself what I was doing to build the ruins of others so they can be comfortable. In verse 5 the Lord says, *"Give careful thought to your ways."*

1. Verse 6 He continues, *"You have planted much, but harvested little. Can I see God's house being built and not just my own? Who am I bringing to my Father's House?"*
2. *"You eat, but never have enough."* Am I feeding others in this house?
3. *"You drink, but never have your fill."* Am I serving others? Am I filling their glasses?
4. *"You put on clothes, but are not warm."* Do I clothe others?
5. *"You earn wages, only to put them in a purse with holes in it."* Do I spend my money to help others?

Then God continues on in verses 7 and 8, *"Give careful thought to your ways. Go up into the mountains and bring down timber..."* It made me think that things are never easy and may not be something I will understand or even like, but I must go and obey the opportunities God gives to me to build His house, or His people, in any way He sees fit with any means I may have.

He says in verse 9, *"'You expected much but see it turned out to be little. What you brought home, I blew away. Why?' declares the Lord Almighty. 'Because of my house, which remains a ruin, while each of you is busy with your own house.'"*

Kids, the message here is that sometimes we work so hard for all the wrong things, and in the end it amounts to nothing. It will blow away just like the wind blows the leaves off the trees and then they die. We must not become so busy with our own home and its comforts that we forget God's house needs to be built as well. His house is a house that we can invite others into. It is a house with a big, big yard, with lots and lots of food for everyone. God has blessed us so much. May we never come to the place where we cannot see beyond our own house. God's house is a big, big house designed to have more than enough of everything for all who come. This is just a challenge for us to not forget others.

Love you all,

Mom

"Do You See Me?"

Good Morning Children,

As you know I have returned from Africa, yet I am not the same. Each time I go to serve others, God teaches more of who He is to me. I have come home different and more in love with Jesus than before. Sometimes we can become too used to the way things are in our faith. We live our lives, and for the most part we stay closed off. We don't want to be seen because if people knew who we really were, they may not like us. We put on our masks and hide. Why is that?

I was in a conference with 3,500 women who are considered the outcasts of all outcasts. The ones no one wanted…especially the Church. They were the prostitutes, the disease infected, the smelly, and the dirty. They were the ones with worn clothes, the ones with sores on their feet, their heads and all over their bodies. And yet these were the very people Jesus was with and longed to set free.

I watched as these most beautiful women loved God with all their heart, with all their soul and with all their minds. They came because they wanted to come to Jesus. To a place where they were invited to come to, a place of acceptance, a place of being touched, a place of being loved and a place of hope. They came and they gave themselves to worship through dance, through tears, through gut wrenching repentance and confession.

God's word became alive to me. The stories He told were being lived out before my eyes. One of the stories the Lord taught us was about the sinful woman in Luke 7:36-50. In verse 44, Jesus asks, *"Do you see this woman?"* Sounds like a strange question for Jesus to ask, seeing how this Pharisee had already seen this woman come into his house, crying, weeping and washing Jesus' feet. After watching her, and judging her and Jesus, he said if he knew what kind of woman she was, a sinner, and if Jesus knew that he would not touch her. The problem was that even though he saw the woman physically; he did not truly see her. He had no idea who she was.

Jesus allowed me to see this woman and many like her in the conference. I was so humbled and honored to be in their presence. They came to Jesus and they did not care who saw them, they knew that Jesus saw them. They had realized how much they had done and knew only Jesus could forgive them. They had walked from miles and miles away. They came out of the bush. They came so filled with hurt, pain and rejection. When they came to Him, they came not with a cry, but a wail so deep it penetrated the very depths of their inner being.

Jesus told a story to Simon. Two people owed a debt, both were unable to pay. One owed a large debt and one a small debt. Both debts were forgiven. He posed the question, *"Now which of them will love him more?"* He replied, *"I suppose the one who had the bigger debt forgiven"* (Luke 7:42-43). This woman has loved much. For he who has been forgiven little, loves little and those who have been forgiven much, love much. Then Jesus said to the woman, *"Your sins are forgiven...Your faith has saved you; go in peace"* (Verses 48-50). It wasn't what she did that saved her, it was her faith.

Kids, may we never ever forget where we have come from. Because when we do we begin to be like the Pharisee who only notices the sins of others rather than seeing them the way Jesus sees them. May we never forget we have been forgiven much and may we love deeply all the more.

Mom

"Judging Others"

Good Morning Children,

This morning I am thinking about the judgments we make each day. We judge the hearts of others as if we are the one who made their heart. We have no idea where or what others have been going through that make them do the things they do. I would like to tell you a story. It is a story of a six year old little girl. She did not know her father and her mother, who was all she had, because they died with HIV AIDS. She wandered around digging in the trash for food and she drank from the water in the streets. Someone found her and used her for prostitution. She was scared, hurt and she cried. No place to go, she lived under the oppression of the man who said he would kill her if she left. When she was old enough and became pregnant, she was forced to abort over and over. She received beatings for not performing enough. The people in the town knew her as the prostitute; she was looked down on, talked about and laughed at. To them she was trash.

I want you to know I saw her at the conference. Someone invited her to a place where she was accepted and loved. Someone showed her Jesus. She stood before over 3,000 people and shared her life for the first time. She was so full of shame that her whole body shook. She cried, pleading for God to forgive her. So, was she a prostitute? Prostitution is what she was made to do, but it was not who she was.

What if the child in this story was your child? This was God's child. He loves her so much. Sometimes we never take the time to see people and the hurt they carry with them. We judge actions without discernment. I know I have judged people based on their actions, but the fact is I don't know what they have been through. And some of the people I have judged. I have found that I myself have been guilty of the same thing.

So what does the Bible say about judging others? Matthew 7:1-5 tells us, *"Do not judge, or you too will be judged. For in the same way you judge others, you will be judged, and with the measure you use, it will be measured to you. Why do you look at the speck of sawdust in your brother's eye and pay no attention to the plank in your own eye? How can you say to you brother, 'Let me take the speck out of your eye,' when all the time there is a plank in your own eye? You hypocrite, first take the plank out of your own eye, and then you will see clearly to remove the speck from your brother's eye."*

Romans 14:13 says, *"Therefore let us stop passing judgment on one another. Instead, make up your mind not to put any stumbling block or obstacle in the way of a brother or sister."*

Lord, give us eyes today to see your children who need love and acceptance. Amen.

I love you all,

Mom

"Dancing with God"

Good Morning Children,

Africa was an amazing trip, but I cannot stop thinking about the dance. I have never danced that way before, and yet it was not your normal dance. It was a release of the spirit and soul, an incredible freedom and joy, and a time to dance before the Lord. As I was thinking about the dance this morning I read in Psalm 30:10-12, *"Hear, Lord, and be merciful to me; Lord, be my help. You turned my wailing into dancing; you removed my sackcloth and clothed me with joy, that my heart may sing your praises and not be silent. Lord my God, I will praise you forever."*

It hit me why this dancing was so powerful. Kids, the ladies we ministered to were in such pain, such oppression, and hardship. They were ladies that had nothing. Ladies that cried out to God from their innermost being with loud wails. God takes away their pain and what does God clothe them with? JOY! Joy is better than anything you could ever clothe yourself with. We try so hard to mask our pain with stuff, but joy is the true remedy for our pain and sorrow. We must give the soul that weeps and wails a way to release. This release is found in the dance. During the dance in Africa, we shouted and sang to God. We laughed and I can never remember a time that my soul was so filled with greater joy. At the end of the conference, I thanked the Africans for teaching me to dance, for teaching me how to express and release myself to God in such a beautiful way. The dance is not in a move, but in an attitude of the heart, that says, *"God, I want you to fill my pain and longing with you."*

David writes in the beginning of Psalm 30, *"I will exalt you, Lord, for you lifted me out of the depths and did not let my enemies gloat over me. Lord my God, I called to you for help, and you healed me. You, Lord, brought me up from the realm of the dead; you spared me from going down to the pit. Sing the praises of the Lord, you his faithful people; praise his holy name. For his anger lasts only a moment, but his favor lasts a lifetime; weeping may stay for the night, but rejoicing comes in the morning."*

Shall we dance?

I love you,

Mom

"The Harvest"

Good Morning Children,

During our first few days in Africa, we visited some townships where the Horizon drop in centers are located. Driving along the long dusty roads, I noticed children carrying or using a wheel barrow to carry containers of water. As we approached the drop in center, a lot of people were lined up to get water from the well, but as we visited and played with the kids, I came to the realization that most of the team were holding empty water bottles. About four kids were looking at the bottles and I asked if they wanted them. *"YES!"* they replied. Then I watched them run over to the well where the other children were getting a drink with their hands and they filled up the bottles. I didn't even think about them not having something to drink from. What was trash to me was treasure to them.

I certainly have taken for granted that I have clean water every day, not only to drink, but to bathe in. I have learned that thousands of children and adults die due to lack of clean water. There are so many needs everywhere and this made me understand a little more why Jesus said in Matthew 9:35-38, *"Jesus went through all the towns and villages, teaching in their synagogues, proclaiming the good news of the kingdom and healing every disease and sickness. When he saw the crowds, he had compassion on them, because they were harassed and helpless, like sheep without a shepherd. Then he said to his disciples, "The harvest is plentiful but the workers are few. Ask the Lord of the harvest, therefore, to send out workers into his harvest field."*

I know this is Dad's passion. It is what he does. Taking people to where the harvest is ripe, where as far as your eyes can see there are fields full of the harassed, helpless and innocent. A field full of injustice and suffering beyond even our ability to understand. A field ripe for the harvest.

Love you all,

Mom

"Who is My Neighbor?"

Good Morning Children,

I was reading this morning in Proverbs 14:20, *"The poor are shunned even by their neighbors…"* It made me think of one of the most impactful moments on our trip in Africa. One day we went to a very nice shopping area to get food and water. Very few poor people were around. As we were being dropped off I saw an African woman holding a baby. She seemed to be wondering around in a daze. I noticed how people were just passing her by. The thoughts going through my head were, *"I hope someone helps her. What can I do? I'm only here for a moment. What would she think if I approached her? I'm a stranger."*

Ignoring my thoughts I entered the store, but could not get her out of my mind. I went back outside and saw her sitting alone. I came up next to her and without words I sat down and took her hand. Tears welled up in both of our eyes. I took off my cross and placed it around her neck, and told her God loved her. She clung to that cross. I remembered they had a stand in front of the grocery store selling tortillas. I went to get her some and when I brought them back she clapped her hands together to say thank you. I gave her the money I had and she smiled and then it was time to go. I have not told anyone this story because it left me in awe and words could not have expressed God's presence. It was not what I did for that woman, but what that woman did for me.

God is teaching me again who my neighbors are and if I only have five minutes, He can take that small amount of time and use it. My thought this morning is this. I don't want God's love to ever become a duty I have to perform, but rather a love that is birthed out of my relationship with Him that I get to have the pleasure of being a part of.

Love you,

Mom

"Death: God's Secret"

Good Morning Children,

I had the privilege to work in the vegetable gardens with the ladies at the drop in center. Although we pulled weeds all day, we actually did much more. We talked about life in our cultures and laughed together. About the middle of the day, we stopped working and sat together and just shared with each other. It was wonderful and so peaceful. I learned that a woman named Faith had just buried her husband. Here is what she talked to me about concerning death…

> *"Death is God's secret because we don't know when we are going to pass away. If we knew, we would live sad and not enjoy life. Because we are surrounded by death, I tell the children to trust God because when He took their parents, He had a purpose. He's the only one who knows why He took them. It was their hour to go home with Jesus."*

Mark 13:32 says, *"But about that day or hour no one knows, not even the angels in heaven, nor the Son, but only the Father."* Deuteronomy 29:29 says this about death, *"The secret things belong to the Lord our God…"*

I have thought a lot about what Faith said to me. None of us know for sure when God will whisper in our ears, *"It's time to come home."* It has made me think more about how I live and love. So before today passes, I want you all to know, while I am not perfect, I love you with all my heart.

Your wife and Mom

My Daughter-In-Laws Response to "Death: God's Secret"

I really liked your message about "death". I was thinking about it when I drove home from work last night. It is amazing how God knows exactly what He is doing by making our lives, yet the timing of our death remains a mystery. We never would live our lives out to the fullest if we knew when we were going to die and experience some of the amazing things we are so blessed to experience while we are here on earth. I thought for instance, *"What if I knew something tragic was going to happen to my husband while we were young? Would I have ever married him and experienced sharing so many amazing moments together? What if I knew that I would get cancer as a young mother and die? Would I ever have the courage to have children and experience the blessing of being a mother to my daughter?"*

I think we would live in constant fear and never have hope or ambition to do anything. Knowing about death would be a hindrance to God's great plans. I think about all my patients and the death I experience all of the time working as a nurse. Though they are diagnosed with a terminal disease they still have no set "date" when they will leave this place. I see them still fighting, still hoping, still trusting in God that their days will be far from over. Not knowing our time of death allows us to rely on God and to trust in Him. His mysteries and design of human life never cease to amaze me. Thanks for sharing your thoughts. It is awesome to learn from the women of Africa through you, even though I have never even been there!

Love you,

Tammy

Jason and Tammy

"Death"

Good Morning Children,

I talked to my granddaughter this week and our conversation went somewhat like this... *"Nana, my bunny died on my birthday."* *"Ayla,"* I replied, *"I remember when my grandma died on my birthday. I really thought it was special because she went to heaven on my birthday. It was kind of her first birthday in heaven."* *"Well, Nana my bunny did not go to heaven,"* she said. *"Yes, she did,"* I responded. *"No! She didn't Nana. I put her right in the ground! She did not go to heaven!"* she insisted.

Well, I dare you to try to explain anymore. One of the things people often ask is, *"What happens to me when I die?"* It is interesting that in Bible study we have been studying this very question. Jesus often spoke of those who died as being "asleep". 1 Thessalonians 4:13-14 states, *"Brothers and sisters, we do not want you to be uninformed about those who sleep in death, so that you do not grieve like the rest of mankind, who have no hope. For we believe that Jesus died and rose again, and so we believe that God will bring with Jesus those who have fallen asleep in him."* The scripture says to be absent from the body is to be present with the Lord. The thief who hung on the cross was told by Jesus in Luke 23:43, *"... today you will be with me in paradise."* 1 Thessalonians 4:16-18 tells us that when this body dies, or falls asleep, our spirit goes right away to be with the Lord. There will be a day when an alarm clock will go off and those bodies that have fallen asleep in the Lord will rise to meet Him in the air and so shall we ever be with the Lord.

So what about bunnies? What would heaven be like without bunnies? If the lion can lay down with the lambs, I know heaven would include

Ayla's bunny. Rejoice because all of your names are written in the Book of Life.

I love you,

Mom

"Until Death Do We Part"

Good Morning Children,

I was reading the story of Stephen's life in Acts 6-7. He was chosen to serve with the apostles because he was a man full of faith and the Holy Spirit. Full of God's grace and power. He also did great wonders and miraculous signs among the people. Because of this the religious people feared losing their power. They brought false accusations against him. They brought Stephen before them and he declared with boldness the truth including a strong rebuke to them calling them *"stiff-necked people! Your hearts and ears are still uncircumcised"* (Acts 7:51). They were furious and at that moment heaven opened and there was Jesus standing at the right hand of God. *"Look!"* Stephen said, *"I see the heaven open and the son of man standing at the right hand of God"* (Acts 7:56). But they covered their ears, rushed him and dragged him out into the city where they proceeded to stone him to death. Stephen was crying out to the Lord not to hold this sin against them.

After reading this I thought of the faithfulness of Stephen's life. Even in the face of death his message never changed. It inspired me to be a stronger witness for God and to proclaim the message of Jesus to others. Sometimes I am hindered because I wonder what others will think of me. Even to the very end, Stephen was thinking of others, even those who opposed him. One day, Kids, we will no longer have a voice to proclaim the great news of Jesus to others. In the end it really doesn't matter what others think of us. Or does it? Will they say we were faithful to the end?

I pray for all of us this morning that we will be strong in the face of those who oppose the truth and that with boldness we will proclaim the wonderful name of Jesus...until death do we part!

Love you all,

Mom

"The Gatekeeper"

Good Morning Children,

I remember entering the Mantipane Village and pulling up to the care center where we were going to serve. It was surrounded by a large gate. We waited as a man came with the keys and unlocked it for us. I would later learn this man's name was Earnest. His presence made you feel so special and welcome. He would make the ladies on the team feel as if we were queens and each time he would see any of us he would place his hands together and bow his head. He worked as hard or even harder than anyone alongside of us at making sure we had what we needed. When I think of him I think of a gatekeeper, a monitor or overseer. One who is entrusted with keys or someone who controls access to an area he protects. He became a picture of the heart of Jesus to me. Once we entered through the gate, I think all of us knew we were on Holy Ground. It made me think of the great privilege we have of being counted worthy enough to enter through the gate, which was made possible through Jesus.

In John 10:9-10, Jesus said, *"I am the gate; whoever enters through me will be saved. They will come in and go out, and find pasture...I have come that they may have life, and have it to the full."* In the midst of great suffering, disease, and poverty was an opportunity and a privilege to enter in. The gateway Earnest opened to us that day was a pasture full of peace, laughter, unity and pure joy. It was where life had meaning and was being lived out in its fullest. I am so thankful and grateful that we all have the privilege and access of being a part of God's pasture. We all have entered through Jesus, the only gateway to life. In some ways we all have been given a set of keys, ones that open life to our family, friends and neighbors. Like Earnest, we all are the keeper of the keys.

Love you all,

Mom

"I Get to..."

Good Morning Children,

This morning we will wake up to many things we have to do.

> *I have to go to work.*
> *I have to take care of the kids.*
> *I have to clean and do laundry.*
> *I have to meet with my friends.*
> *I have a meeting I have to go to.*
> *I have to do my devotions and pray.*
> *Or if you have kids they may say…do I have to???*

I would like to tell you a story of a little girl I was with in Africa. Each day, as a part of the VBS we conducted, the kids would have rotations they would do. Bible story, sports, and a craft. At the end of all the rotations we would all gather together for a time of singing and dancing before the Lord. I was one of the people leading the sports and it was time to gather together. We started up the hill towards the area where we met when a little girl came running up to me and grabbed my hand to pull me towards the meeting area.

Isaiah 11:6 says, *"…a little child will lead them."* She looked up at me and said, *"We get to go worship God. We get to sing to God. We get to love God."* She was so excited! So many times we look at life and worship as something we have to do, a responsibility, as opposed to the thing we get to do or a privilege. What would happen if we started thinking differently about the things we do? Here is what it would sound like…

I get to be with my kids and spouse.
I get to go to work.
I get to be with my friends.
I get to go to church and I get to worship, praise and pray.
I get to watch my granddaughter.
I get to go to Nana's.

Life should not become a duty. Today, listen to what you say. I am leaving in just a few minutes, but I get to go to Bible Study and meet with good friends. I get to love today. What a joy!

Love,

Mom

"Clapping"

Good Morning Children,

It is a good morning! I was reading the other day in Psalm 47:1-2, *"Clap your hands, all you nations; shout to God with cries of joy. For the Lord Most High is awesome, the great King over all the earth."* I was thinking of why people clap their hands. I clap my hands when someone has done a good job. I clap my hands when I get excited. I clap my hands to the beat of a song.

I called my granddaughters to ask why they clap their hands. Addi, the older one, said, *"When I am happy and want to show my appreciation for someone."* Ayla said, *"I clap for clowns. They are funny."* I guess we clap for many reasons.

I remember while in Zimbabwe we were giving food to the children, but before they would take food from you they would clap their hands to say thank you. I had to ask myself, *"When do I clap just for you Lord? The awesome things you have done? For your wonders all around me?"* So for the last couple of days I have been practicing "The Clap" to God. I heard the birds sing, so I clapped. I thought of my granddaughter, and I clapped. I prayed over my food, and I clapped. I will definitely have to say that it made me smile. More than anything I think God wants us to acknowledge Him and the amazing things He has created and gives to us each day. So go ahead and clap! Why should I clap, you ask? Just because of who He is.

Love you all,

Mom

"Our Testimony"

Good Morning Children,

I was reading in Acts this morning about how Paul was thrown into prison for spreading the news about Jesus. He called people everywhere to repent and believe in His name. I admire his dedication and boldness even though he faced great criticism from others and risked losing his life. Time after time, God placed him in positions where he could share his testimony with those in great authority and surrounded by great crowds. Paul always looked at what happened in his life as an opportunity to share the Gospel. If God allowed him to go to prison it was for a purpose. That was why he could sing while in chains.

As I began to think about Paul's life, I thought of my own. When I first got saved I was filled with joy and boldly proclaimed that people should repent and believe in the name of Jesus. I was a bartender at the time and carried the Bible with me to work. I shared passionately about Jesus, but what you have to understand is that my whole life up until that point was lived without any knowledge of God's word. I did not go to church and had never even read the Bible. All I knew, Kids, was that I was introduced to Jesus. I had made a confession of my belief in Him and invited Him into my life. Supernaturally I was filled with a love I had never experienced before and I just had to share it with others. I never want to forget that there is a whole world of people out there that are just like I was…Lost!

The last verse in Acts 28:31 Paul welcomed all who came to see him. Boldly and without hindrance he preached the kingdom of God and taught about the Lord Jesus Christ.

People are not impressed with how much you know until they know what you've lived. Share your testimony.

I love you,

Mom

"Guarding"

Good Morning Children,

"...guard what has been entrusted to your care" (1 Timothy 6:20).

As I read this verse, I thought about my granddaughter, Norah. Each Monday my son Jason brings her over and he hands her over to me as if to say, *"Mom, I am entrusting my little girl to you today. I trust you to guard her, care for her, love her and protect her."* I do not take this responsibility lightly. She is always with Dad or me and I am always mindful of what she is learning while in my care. There is never a time I don't know where she is or what she is doing. Even as she sleeps I am peeking in on her. I never thought of myself as a guard, but that is what I am.

As I looked at Timothy's life I learned three things about him and am inspired by them.

1. Acts 16:1 shows that Timothy's mom was a believer.
2. In 2 Timothy 1:5, it was his grandma and his mom that instilled in him a sincere faith.
3. 2 Timothy 3:15 shows that from infancy he was taught the scriptures.

Now he has received this charge from Paul to guard all those things that have been entrusted to him. To care for the church and teach others God's word. Those things that had been planted in him from the time he was an infant.

I have been challenged as I ask myself these three questions. What have I been entrusted with? How well am I guarding it? How much do I care about it?

Thanking God for His grace,

Mom

"If or When"

Good Morning Children,

I finally get it Jason and Josh! I have always remembered the day I was helping you with your homework. It was a math problem, which went something like this…

> IF Johnny went to the store and bought 8 apples and on the way home he lost 3, how many apples would Johnny have?

To me the answer was simple, 5. But it was not simple to you. *"It's a trick question Mom because we don't know if Johnny really went. Why doesn't it just say, 'WHEN' Johnny went instead of 'IF' then we would know for sure?"* After many tears your dad finally arrived home and we told him the question and without hesitation he said, *"We don't really know IF Johnny went or not."* I couldn't believe it. I could not see it. You both refused to answer the question.

I was thinking this morning about those who are hurting, those who are hungry, and those who are sick and lonely. There are so many. Like your math problem, it should not be a question of "*if*" we become involved, but a question of "*when*". Jesus said to the righteous in Matthew 25:35-36, *"For I was hungry and you gave me something to eat, I was thirsty and you gave me something to drink, I was a stranger and you invited me in, I needed clothes and you clothed me, I was sick and you looked after me, I was in prison and you came to visit me."* It was not an IF question. Then the righteous asked in verses 37-39, *"Lord, WHEN did we see you hungry and feed you, or thirsty and give you something to drink? WHEN did we see you a stranger and invite you in, or needing clothes and clothe you? WHEN*

91

did we see you sick or in prison and go to visit you?" Jesus replied in verse 40, *"Truly I tell you, whatever you did for one of the least of these brothers and sisters of mine, you did for me."* It was an absolute!

What I love about this is that the righteous were doing what they knew to be right and did not even know WHEN they did these things they were doing it to Jesus himself. To them it was not about getting praise or rewards, it was about loving because they had been given love. Selfless love. The very nature of God birthed in them. Kids, action is better than apathy.

God help us to see WHEN Jesus is hurting and to be active in loving Him through your people every day and every way.

I love you,

Mom

"The Field of God"

Good Morning Children,

When you think of a field, what is the first thing that comes to mind? I asked this question to people all day at work. Wind blowing through tall grass, flowers, wheat, corn...etc. Almost everyone saw a field that was empty. I asked people this question because I was reading this morning about the field that God sees. My study took me many places in the Word. I'd like to share the questions I asked the Lord.

> What is the field you see Lord? Matthew 13:38 tells us, *"The field is the world..."*

> Who is in your field? 1 Corinthians 3:9 says, *"...you are God's field, God's building."*

> What do you want me to see in this field? John 4:35 instructs us, *"I tell you, open your eyes and look at the fields! They are ripe for harvest."*

God has assigned us a portion of His field to work in right where we are each day. Jesus talked about God's field in Matthew 9:35-38. He said he saw people who were hurting, harassed, and helpless. He had compassion on them. Then he says in verses 37-38, *"The harvest is plentiful but the workers are few. Ask the Lord of the harvest, therefore, to send out workers into his harvest field."*

Wherever we are kids, we are in God's field. A field that isn't empty, but full of people who need Him. People who are hurting, helpless and harassed. It's harvest time!

I love you,

Mom

"It's Harvest Time"

Good Morning Children,

One of my favorite times of the year is spring. Everything is coming up and new life can be seen in the flowers, trees and the little birds singing and flying around. Well several weeks ago, I had the opportunity to see spring early. Although it was different, it was still filled with new life. Your dad was asked to speak at an inner city church in downtown Indianapolis called Brookside. It was one of the most emotional and impactful services I have ever been to. Why? Because what had not been seen was revealed.

I recall when your dad heard the Lord speak to him about partnering with this church and how God led him every step of the way to a man called Bob, who had an after school ministry for kids. Dad shared with Bob what God had spoken to him and how he would like to partner with him to help the kids. Bob told him he had been praying for several years for God to send him someone. I remember like it was yesterday Dad meeting with our friends, John and Barbie, in their home to ask them to go down and begin working with Bob. And then he met with our other friends Aaron and Beth about partnering in this work. It was a divine appointment in God's plan for the direction of their lives. Aaron introduced Dad that day as the patriarch of Brookside and Dad came and shared the story of how Brookside became a church.

It hit me how what was planted years ago had now sprouted up to so many people being involved and how many souls had been saved. The church was full and the song of praise to God filled the air. I thought to myself, *"This is harvest time."* So many people had planted and now the harvest was plainly visible. As I looked around at the fruit of your dad's obedience I was so proud of him and the way God had led him.

Galatians 6:9-10 says, *"Let us not become weary in doing good, for at the proper time we will reap a harvest if we do not give up. Therefore, as we have opportunity, let us do good to all people, especially to those who belong to the family of believers."*

Whatever God is speaking to you today, Kids, endure its hardships because what you cannot see today will become visible tomorrow.

Love to all,

Mom

"Psalm 66:16"

Good Morning Children,

"Come and hear, all you who fear God; let me tell you what he has done for me" (Psalm 66:16). What has He done just for me? As I thought about this I had to go back to the beginning because everything He has done has been birthed out of that moment. That personal moment where God met me right where I was. He came to me, Sandra Mae Mode, and I know He knew my name and all I had ever done. I was in such need of someone to love me just for me. I was headed down a path that would have ended in a life filled with pain. I was looking for love in all the wrong places. But, God, in His mercy, saw me. He offered me a life of being loved, not a life free from troubles, but a life knowing that whatever I will go through He is there with me and will never leave. A life filled with purpose and with great love.

How did this happen? I am in awe. How could one person change a life totally in a moment? How great is that love that He could reach down to a hurting young woman and touch her in such a way that she knew she was loved? I recall a peace I had never felt and an overwhelming presence that filled my whole being. Amazing, miraculous, unexplainable, incomprehensible...His love set me free. So when I think of this question, I think God has done everything for me. I want to spend the rest of my life saying thank you and asking Him the question, *"What is it Lord that I can do for you?"*

Love you all so much,

Mom

"The Power of Holding Sin over Someone's Life"

Good Morning Children,

I have been following a story on CNN about a teacher who was approached by a student that told her, *"I know who you are and what you did."* This student found some pictures of her posing nude when she was 20. She is now in her 40's. CNN was asking the question, *"Should this woman be allowed to continue teaching, or be dismissed?"* Yesterday, she came out and explained that when she was 21 she worked in a strip club. She was poor and needed the money. She admitted she made a lot of bad choices, but she worked her way out of that lifestyle and pursued her dream of becoming a teacher. She put herself through school and finally accomplished her dream. She said, *"I love teaching and I have been doing it for many years. I have not been involved in any sexual misconduct since my youth."*

I hurt for this woman. All that ran through my mind was that I hope to God that no one ever pulls up what I did when I was 20. It made me think of the woman in John 8 who was caught in adultery and taken into the streets to be stoned. Jesus replied to the Pharisees in verse 7, *"Let any one of you who is without sin be the first to throw a stone at her."* Everyone went away. Then Jesus turned to the woman and said in verses 10-11, *"'Woman, where are they? Has no one condemned you?' 'No one, sir,' she said. 'Then neither do I condemn you,' Jesus declared. 'Go now and leave your life of sin.'"*

Here is a woman who left her life of sin and turned it around and yet she is still being drug into the streets. Yes, our choices do have a huge impact on our lives, and some of the sin's we commit have huge consequences. Although, this teacher did not commit a criminal offense, the power of her sin still remained over her.

Kids, I want to encourage you today to first live a life with full knowledge that what you do affects not only you, but everyone in relation to you. One act, one decision can be made in a moment and yet last for a lifetime and can affect generations to come. Second, never hold a sin over someone's head after they have turned from it. Often time's people struggle to be free because they are reminded constantly of it, therefore, they remain in bondage. Third, if someone confides in you it means they trust you. Don't betray them by sharing with others their struggles. The power of holding sin over someone's life is unforgiveness. Forgive!

I love you,

Mom

"The Lap of God"

Good Morning Children,

As I was reading Psalm 78 this morning I thought of when you all were little and would crawl up onto my lap. A lot of things happened. You would take a load off your feet. You would lay your chest on mine. You had my attention because I was sitting down, which was a miracle in and of itself. It was in those times we would talk.

The Psalmist is expressing in verse 4 how important it is to *tell the next generation the praiseworthy deeds of the Lord, his power, and the wonders he has done.* Verses 5-7 show the importance of teaching our children God's laws so that the next generation will know His laws and not forget his deeds and keep his commands. The chapter goes on to recall God's faithfulness to Israel in the midst of severe circumstances. Most of them only saw their situation; they complained, they demanded, they were fearful and unfaithful. They called out in verses 19-20, *"Can God really spread the table in the wilderness? … Can he supply meat for his people?"* God caused water to gush out of a rock and He opened the heavens and it rained down food.

This morning you may have many concerns. How can I provide? Will I have enough? …etc. I want to remind you that God is able and He is enough! Trust in Him and not your circumstances. Recall those times in the past where He has proven Himself faithful. And then give thanks!

Although my lap is too small for you to sit on now, I want you to remember that the *"Lap of God"* is always available. He is always there to take your load, to pick you up and talk. I would also like to encourage you to take the most of every opportunity to instill in your children, the next generation, the faithfulness of God.

I love you!

Mom

"Struggling with Sin?"

Good Morning Children,

In Romans chapter 6, Paul was talking about the issue of sin. He reminds us that when we accept Christ, sin should no longer be a master over us. As I was reading I thought about Star Wars. Two powers at war, two masters and two sides. Both trying to take control or lure one to the dark side or the good side. The reason I thought about this is because in verse 14 it says, *"For sin shall no longer be your master"*. Darth Vader was the master that represented the rebellion. The dark side was always trying to lure others from the good side.

Paul talks about this dark side, or sin. He asked the church in verse 21, *"What benefit did you reap at that time from the things you are now ashamed of? Those things result in death!"* One word throughout this whole chapter stood out to me. The word OFFER appears five times. Verse 13, *"Do not OFFER any part of yourself to sin as an instrument of wickedness, but rather OFFER yourselves to God…"* Verse 16 says, *"Don't you know that when you OFFER yourselves to someone as obedient slaves, you are slaves of the one you obey…"* And verse 19 states, *"Just as you used to OFFER yourselves as slaves to impurity and to ever-increasing wickedness, so now OFFER yourselves as slaves to righteousness leading to holiness."*

It became clear to me. It's about OFFERING. Who do you offer yourself to each day? Lord and Master, I OFFER myself and my family to you today.

Love you all!

Mom

"Freedom"

Good Morning Children,

What is it that you have done that keeps you in bondage? Have you cried out for peace and forgiveness, offering to exchange your past for a fresh start? I was reading the story of the sinful woman today in Luke 7:36-50. Here is a woman who wanted her past forgiven and she went to great lengths to find forgiveness. She was ridiculed when she pursued a relationship with Jesus. She didn't need a physical healing like so many others did. She needed an inner healing. Others held her in bondage, and in this case it was the ones in the church. They said of her, *"If this man were a prophet, he would know who is touching him and what kind of woman she is – that she is a sinner."* Religious people of that day didn't want anyone who was a sinner to be around. Even today religious people still hold people outside when they should be the very ones bringing them inside.

Jesus used a story of two men that owed money, one owed five hundred denarii and the other one fifty denarii. Neither one of them had the money to pay their debt, but both debts were cancelled. Jesus posed a question in verse 42, *"Now which of them will love him more?" "I suppose the one who had a bigger debt forgiven,"* was their reply. He pointed out that none of the religious people acknowledged him, but this woman had. Then he made this statement in verse 47, *"…her great love has shown. But whoever has been forgiven little loves little."* Then he continues in verses 48-50 to tell the woman, *"Your sins are forgiven…Your faith has saved you; go in peace."*

Ahh, the peace of having your sins forgiven. That Kids, is true peace. Freedom from condemnation and guilt. Another verse came to mind as I was reading this story. It is found in John 1:29, *"Look, the lamb of God, who takes away the sin of the world!"* Jesus has the power to take away our sins. No more bondage, and no more guilt. We have only one response, to love much and forgive as you have been forgiven for we all have had our debts paid in full. To God be the Glory!

With much love,

Mom

"Endurance"

Good Morning Children,

This morning I would like to ask you a question. How well are you enduring what life has given you? To understand this question a little better I looked up the word *endurance*. According to www.dictionary.com it is defined as the ability or strength to continue or last, especially despite fatigues, stress or other adverse conditions. The power of enduring an unpleasant or difficult situation without giving up, bearing pain or hardship.

I was thinking about what Jesus had to endure on the road to the cross. He was made fun of, ridiculed, spit on and stripped. He was in great pain and fatigue as they laid the cross on Him and placed a crown of thorns upon His head, but He never gave up.

Today in Bible Study we will study 2 Timothy 2. Paul is chained in prison as he speaks these words in verse 3, *"Join with me in suffering..."* He continues in verses 8-10, *"Remember Jesus Christ, raised from the dead, descended from David. This is my gospel, for which I am suffering even to the point of being chained like a criminal. But God's word is not chained. Therefore I endure everything for the sake of the elect, that they too may obtain the salvation that is in Christ Jesus, with eternal glory."*

This is our gospel as well. Jesus Christ came into our world, died and was resurrected. It was a great sacrifice. This morning you may be going through a tough time. Only God knows the thoughts of our hearts. My prayer for you and myself this morning is for endurance. That we may consider Christ in anything we are going through and find strength and joy in Him to endure so that no one is left to wonder who we serve. *"His love endures forever"* (Psalm 136:1).

I love you,

Mom

"Good Friday"

Good Morning Children,

Today is the day we remember the death of Christ. As I thought about Good Friday and what it means to me, I thought about how His death is still teaching me how to die every day. His life taught us how to live by dying to the very things we think give us life. By doing the very things he taught us to do. He gave up His power so we could have it. The cross teaches one to love, to give their life for the sake of another. It teaches us to persevere and to have endurance. It reminds me of the joy I have felt as I look in the face of the poor that moves me beyond myself. This great sacrifice paid the price for my sinfulness and paved a way for me to experience life no matter what it may bring. The cross is my hope, what I base the foundation of my life on. His death gave me life, purpose and forgiveness. To God be the Glory forever and ever.

Jesus talks about His death in John 12:23-28, *"The hour has come for the Son of Man to be glorified. Very truly I tell you, unless a kernel of wheat falls to the ground and dies, it remains only a single seed. But if it dies, it produces many seeds. Anyone who loves their life will lose it, while anyone who hates their life in this world will keep it for eternal life. Whoever serves me must follow me; and where I am, my servant also will be. My Father will honor the one who serves me. Now my soul is troubled, and what shall I say? 'Father, save me from this hour?' No, it was for this very reason I came to this hour. Father, glorify your name!"*

As your mother, it would give me no greater pleasure than to know that when I am gone you will walk in the ways I have taught you. How much greater on this day that we remember what our Lord taught us. That we are walking out the power of the cross.

My heart is filled with Joy,

Mom

"Knowing or Loving"

Good Evening Children,

I was thinking tonight about how knowledge puffs us up, but loving others builds them up. Just because a person knows a lot does not make them an expert, especially when it comes to knowing God's word. The Pharisees knew, or thought they knew, everything there was to know about God. But they did not love others. They used their knowledge to control, criticize and belittle others. Their knowledge taught them how to love themselves for they loved to be heard for their abundant speaking and long prayers. They lived off of their own pride, which caused them to burn with jealousy for anyone that knew more than they did. It caused them to kill the author of the very book from which they learned. The fruit of growing in knowledge is always loving more. Anytime we use the Bible to just grow in knowledge without growing in love or godliness, we are headed for trouble.

In the morning I will go to Bible Study, a place where I love meeting with other women to grow in my walk with God, but the real fruit of my study comes after I leave. How will I choose to live what I have learned?

Good night!

Mom

"World Changers"

Good Morning Children,

Towards the end of Jesus' life on earth, He was sharing with His disciples what was to come in Luke 22. In the very midst of this came a dispute among them. They were arguing over which one of them would be the greatest in the kingdom. What they were saying was similar to this, *"I am better than you and I deserve to have the highest place of honor."* To them it was about position, blessing and honor.

What should have been a time that was directed to think about what was going to happen to Jesus instead was a time they thought only of themselves. I love how Jesus always honors people even in the midst of their selfishness. He could have said, *"Have you not heard or learned anything I have taught you?"* Instead he used it as another teachable moment.

In Matthew 20:26-27 he says, *"...whoever wants to become great among you must be your servant, and whoever wants to be first must be your slave."* But in Luke 22:26-27 he says, *"Instead, the greatest among you should be like the youngest, and the one who rules like the one who serves. For who is greater, the one who is at the table or the one who serves? Is it not the one who is at the table? But I am among you as one who serves."*

The youngest? The ones who are least honored and yet don't care about their position. The ones who love unconditionally. The ones who don't care about disputes about who's better than who. He was teaching them that to be a world changer, they must be a servant. As we prepare today to go into the world, I challenge you and myself to be world changers. Love like the youngest among us.

Love you all,

Mom

"The Power of a Touch"

Good Morning Children,

One day, there was a large crowd that surrounded Jesus. *"And a woman was there who had been subject to bleeding for twelve years. She had suffered a great deal under the care of many doctors and had spent all she had, yet instead of getting better she grew worse. When she heard about Jesus, she came up behind him in the crowd and touched his cloak, because she thought, 'If I just touch his clothes, I will be healed.' Immediately her bleeding stopped and she felt in her body that she was freed from her suffering. At once Jesus realized that power had gone out of him. He turned around in the crowd and asked, 'Who touched my clothes?' 'You see the people crowding against you,' his disciples answered, "and yet you can ask, 'Who touched me?'"* (Mark 5:25-31). Something different happened to this woman and she knew it, she confessed to Jesus and He told her that her faith had healed her (Mark 5:34).

This weekend while we were at Mammoth Cave, some of the family went horseback riding and Dad and I stayed behind with Brody and Ben. A man brought a horse out and gave the boys a little ride. As this man was talking to Dad, I was stroking the horse along the bridge of her nose. With each stroke her eyes slowly shut. Even though four other people were touching her she responded to my touch. I was filled with compassion and I think the way I was touching it brought healing.

Silly? I don't think so. I think anytime you touch with compassion, others know it. Later that night, I had some concerns that were weighing on me. My spirit was heavy. Several of us were sitting around the fire and Jason began to touch my shoulders and back gently. No words were exchanged, but with each stroke my eyes slowly shut. It brought healing. We can feel the power of Jesus' touch through the compassionate touch of others. Think about your touch today.

Love you bunches!

Mom

"Temptations"

Good Morning Children,

I was doing a study a few days ago on temptation and would like to share it with you.

1. **God does not tempt us with evil.** James 1:13 says, *"When tempted, no one should say, 'God is tempting me.' For God cannot be tempted by evil, nor does he tempt anyone."*

2. **Does the devil tempt?** Jesus was tempted by the devil. In Matthew 4:1 the Devil is called *"The Tempter"*. Other references are 1 Thessalonians 3:5 and Matthew 4:5.

3. **What part are we responsible for?** James 1:14-15 tells us, *"… each person is tempted when they are dragged away by their own evil desire and enticed. Then, after desire has conceived, it gives birth to sin; and sin, when it is full-grown, gives birth to death."*

4. **Being tempted is not sinning, but giving into temptation is the sin.** Hebrews 4:15, *"For we do not have a high priest who is unable to empathize with our weaknesses, but we have one who has been tempted in every way, just as we are – yet he did not sin."*

5. **You are not alone.** 1 Corinthians 10:13 says, *"No temptation has overtaken you except what is common to mankind."*

6. **God is faithful and He will not let you be tempted beyond what you can bear, but when you are tempted He will also provide a way out so that you can stand up under it.** 1 Corinthians 10:13 says, *"And God is faithful; he will not let you be tempted beyond what you can bear. But when you are tempted, he will also provide a way out so that you can endure it."*

7.   **We find help with others.** James 5:16 instructs us, *"Therefore confess your sins to each other and pray for each other…"*

This morning if you are struggling with being tempted or you find yourself giving into the things that are tempting you, I would like to encourage you with the words from John 8:34. *"Jesus replied, 'Very truly I tell you, everyone who sins is a slave to sin."* You end up serving whatever it is that you give yourself to. It becomes your master and controls you. Jesus provides us a way out. His truth. He says in James 4:7, *"Submit yourselves, then, to God. Resist the devil, and he will flee from you."* I am praying for all of us this morning, that in every way and every day we will glorify His name with the way we live our lives.

I love you,

Mom

"*Distinctions*"

Good Morning Children,

This morning I was reading the story of Moses appearing before Pharaoh. (Exodus Chapters 7-12) One word stood out to me several times. The word "distinction". God said in Exodus 8:23, *"I will make a distinction between my people and your people."* A distinction between those who believe and those who do not. I looked up the word www.dictionary.com and the definition is *"the recognizing or noting of differences; discrimination.* I then asked the Lord, *"What is it that makes a Christian different? Is it because they say they believe in God?"* The scripture says that even the devil believes. Then it must be more. Two scriptures came to mind.

First, we are known by the love we have for one another. Second, we are to love our neighbor as ourselves. The questions I am asking today are, *"How do I love? Do I love because I have to or does this love I have received just overflow out of my life? How do I love and serve those closest to me? My husband, my children, my mother or father, sister, brothers or my neighbor? What would they say? Are there distinctions?"*

Is my love different than the world's love?

Distinctions…

Lord, help us to fall in love so much with you that our lives reflect you to others.

I do love you all. I may not show it all the time. To be honest, I know at times my actions and words do not express or even look like the God I serve. This makes me sad because I have represented Him to others and it is not who He is.

Mom

"A Dwelling Place for God"

Good Morning Children,

Have you really ever thought about the fact that God's home is in you? A place from which He can make His life known unto the world. Colossians 1:27 says, *"…Christ in you, the hope of glory."* Ephesians 2:22 says, *"And in Him you too are being built together to become a dwelling in which God lives by his Spirit."*

How would it change what we do today if you not only knew Christ was with you, but that He lives within you? He knows all we do and the way we do it. Christ chose to dwell there, to go through the tough times of life to offer peace not only to the world, but to us. Colossians 3:16 tells us, *"Let the word of Christ dwell among you **richly** as you teach and admonish one another with all wisdom…"*

Kids, you have heard me say it before, yet I want to say it again. Read God's word! It is a way to release God's power into your life. Nothing, absolutely nothing, can do for you what God's word can. You cannot live in the same home and not communicate with each other. God's word is His way of teaching us, training us, loving us, helping us, and correcting us. It is the most valuable thing in your home…a priceless treasure.

Richly enjoy the company of God's word.

Te Amo Mucho,

Mom

"A Home for God"

Good Morning Children,

Wouldn't you just love to build a home for God? What would you use to build it? What would the outside look like? How about the inside? I would want it to be the best home there ever was. I would use only the best resources to build it, and would work day and night, using all my strength to make it just right. I would want it to be a home where God was proud to live.

In my devotional reading this morning, I read how to build this home. It was not what I would have imagined. Not a building made of wood, nails or block. Not something my human mind would think, but this home is a home that is built within me. A dwelling place not just for Jesus, but for the Father as well. Wow…Me…God's home? The only condition this home required was that it be built on the foundation of love and obedience. It reads like this in John 14:23-24, *"Jesus replied, "Anyone who loves me will obey my teaching. My Father will love them, and we will come to them and make our home with them. Anyone who does not love me will not obey my teaching. These words you hear are not my own; they belong to the Father who sent me."* This instruction manual came from God Himself.

We live in a church age where we are taught to live and love as we choose. If it feels good and makes me happy I will do it. If not, forget it. God's teachings are too hard. *"Thank you God for your grace,"* we say and then live by our own set of instructions.

Kids, this is not about God's love for us, it is about our love for God. Obedience is so important, not even negotiable, to expressing our love to Him. Every home has rules. There were times you broke our house rules. Did we still love you? YES! Sometimes we break God's laws too. We all are guilty, but these are just times to clean the house, whether we like it or not. We must make every effort to obey and honor the Lord in His home. Obedience begins with a desire. Desire the Lord's teaching, impress it on your children. Talk about it to them when you sit at home and when you walk together, when you lie down and when you get up. Write His teachings on the doorframes of your home. (Deuteronomy 6:7)

Nothing is impossible with God!

I love you,

Mom

"Gone Fishing"

Good Morning Children,

Fishing is not something I do very much. To be honest I don't remember when the last time I went fishing. I have been looking at the story in John 21 about fishing. Jesus had just died and his disciples had all decided they would go fishing. In verse 3, Peter says, *"I'm going out to fish." "Hey wait a minute! We'll all go with you. Sounds like fun,"* is how I imagine the other disciples responded. It was fun, until they fished all night and caught not a thing! Jesus, who had resurrected, came to them and said in verses 5-6, *"Friends, haven't you any fish?' 'No,' they answered. 'Throw your net on the right side of the boat and you will find some.' When they did, they were unable to haul the net in because of the large number of fish."* When Peter saw this he knew right away it was the Lord. He was so excited that he jumped into the water and swam to Him. And guess what? Jesus had breakfast waiting.

When they finished eating, Jesus asked the question, *"'Simon son of John, do you love me more than these?'* (What were these? Fish?) *'Yes, Lord,' he said, 'You know that I love you.' Jesus said, 'Feed my lambs.'* (Who are the lambs?) *Again Jesus said, 'Simon son of John, do you love me?' He answered, 'Yes, Lord, you know that I love you.' Jesus said, 'Take care of my sheep.'* (Sheep? What sheep?) *The third time he said to him, 'Simon son of John, do you love me?' Peter was hurt because Jesus asked him the third time, 'Do you love me?' He said, 'Lord, you know all things; you know that I love you.' Jesus said, 'Feed my sheep'"* (Verses 15-17).

So what is this fishing story about? Peter was called to stop fishing and become a fisher of men. Matthew 4:19, *"'Come, follow me,' Jesus said,*

121

'and I will send you out to fish for people.'" But as soon as he thought Jesus was gone he went back to fishing the old way, back to what he knew and was familiar. Maybe he was scared, lost or didn't know what to do. Jesus let him know once again that without Him he could not do anything. So the challenge went out…Ok Peter, do you love me? Do you love me? Do you love me? Then do what I have called you to do. Go fishing where I have called you to fish. Feed my lambs, or in other words take care of my babies. Take care of my sheep, or my people. And feed my sheep! Finally Jesus makes it clear to Him. Follow me.

Sometimes we like the familiar don't we? It is safe! But is it productive? What has God called you to do? Are you doing it? Jesus asks the question to you and to me. Do you love me more than _____? You fill in the blank.

Love you,

Mom

"Adultery"

Good Morning Children,

While we were at Mammoth Cave recently, we did a lot of fun things. My favorite was watching Dad teach the grandkids how to fish. It reminded me a lot of Grandpa teaching all of you at the lake house. At first Addi, had just a stick, no bait or hook on it…or fish for that matter! We found a fishing pole at the little store and some worms. And the fishing began!

Within a minute, Addi caught her first fish. It was as big as your thumb. She was excited because a fish is a fish no matter what size. Then she caught an even bigger fish. The hook was so small that Dad had to cut the head of the fish off to retrieve the hook. That was interesting! Yet as for any good fisherman, the goal became to catch fish. It was a lot of fun.

For the last four days in my Bible study guide my reading has been in Proverbs 5-7. All three chapters are talking about the same things. Adultery and the adulteress. A lot of warnings and consequences. I know…Wait a minute I thought we were talking about fishing?! Well, adultery is a lot like fishing. Something is being sought after and caught, or in danger of being caught.

The fisherman is the enemy, or the Devil, who is continually using bait, or the adulteress, to lure the fish, or you, for his catch. Proverbs uses a strong warning. Stay away! Don't look! Don't take a bite! For if you do death awaits you. You will be yanked out of your environment, gasping for air and not be able to breath. Adultery kills.

I wanted to warn you and encourage you to read these chapters and not only read them, but prepare for them. A lot of times the fisherman is very strategic in his catch. He will not just use worms, crickets, or bread, but he will use other fish as his bait. Fish that look just like you. These are the ones you may work next to, they may be your neighbor, your friends, or sadly enough the one's you worship with. This fisherman has no boundaries. He fishes in the "NO FISHING ZONES".

I leave you with one of the verses that stuck with me. Proverbs 5:21 says, *"For your ways are in full view of the Lord, and he examines all your paths."* Kids, God sees underwater. Live in such a way that allows you to swim freely.

I love you all,

Mom

"Gardening"

Good Morning Children,

One of the things I have enjoyed this summer is working in the yard. In the back there is a beautiful rose bush that I knew I needed to trim because it had a lot of wild branches that stuck out in every direction. I hated trimming it back because it was full of roses. I have learned though that the more I cut it back the more beautiful and uniform it becomes. I have another rose bush that I thought had died last winter. All the branches seemed completely dead, but I noticed a few green leaves right at the base. I decided not to dig it up, but instead decided to cut off all the dead branches and see if it would come back. Guess what? It is growing and has many leaves now. It hasn't produced any roses yet, but I am sure it will in time.

Did you know Jesus called his Father a gardener? Here is what He had to say about gardening in John 15:1-5, *"...my Father is the gardener. He cuts off every branch in me that bears no fruit, while every branch that does bear fruit he prunes so that it will be even more fruitful...No branch can bear fruit by itself; it must remain in the vine. Neither can you bear fruit unless you remain in me. I am the vine; you are the branches. If you remain in me and I in you, you will bear much fruit; apart from me you can do nothing."*

There will be times in your life that you need to be pruned back. It is for your own good and because the Father loves you so much. It is during this time, Kids, that you realize you get your life through being connected to Him. He is our source of life, for no plants survive without roots. He does all of this for one purpose. So that you will glorify His name and that you will bear much fruit in your life (John 15:8).

It's great to be in His garden and know He is taking such good care of us! You all look so beautiful to me! Thank you God for loving my kids!

Mom

"Renewed"

Good Morning Children,

This morning I would like to share with you something that I read yesterday that really renewed me in my spirit. I was reading about Paul approaching his death and his encouragement to Timothy in 2 Timothy 4:6-7. He makes the statement that, *"the time for my departure is near."* Having just been in several airports, I know what departure means. It's time to board, time to go! Paul was getting ready for his last flight. He was reflecting on his life and said, *"I have fought the good fight,"* He had not been in just any fight, but he had been in a good one. He played by the rules. Yes, he got beat up and left for dead at times, but he never gave up. He endured the pain.

I thought to myself, *"I don't just want to have fought in this fight, or be left so beat up that I am staggering around. I want to be left standing strong with a huge smile; even if I have black eyes and blood pouring down my face."* Kids, life is hard and I am sure there are days when you are so beat up and struggling that you don't know if you will have the strength to rise up.

"So how do we fight, Mom?" First, know who you are fighting. It is not your boss, friend, husband or wife, or the person driving in front of you. It is the enemy who uses others at times to attack you. Keep in mind that the enemy does not respect the people he is going to use to get to you. The only way you can fight is to hold on to the Lord. The battle is not yours, but the Lord's. Stay in His word and gain his strength to stand up to the blows of life.

Second, stop fighting for yourself, for your selfish desires, because they will always win. It wants its own way and plays by its own rules. Philippians 2:3 says, *"Do nothing out of selfish ambition or vain conceit. Rather, in humility value others above yourselves…"*

He said, *"I have finished the race."* Dad said he used to tell his carpenters, *"It's not how you start, but how you finish."* Most of us start our relationship with the Lord well, but as soon as it gets hard we often run out of breath and quit. My advice would be to run your race at your own pace. Paul isn't saying win the race, but finish well. Take the time to work on your relationship with the Lord and with others. Don't try to keep up with everyone else. The key to what Paul said is that he kept the faith. He knew God's path was the only one to stay on.

So, I am renewed. I want to finish well. I want you to know I am very glad God allowed me to run with all of you. You all are my teammates!

I love you,

Mom

Never stop striving…
Never stop running…
Never stop believing…

"Renewed: Part 2"

Good Morning Children,

As I was reading the second part of Paul's departure, a statement hit me that he made in 2 Timothy 4:8. *"Now there is in store for me the crown of righteousness, which the Lord, the righteous Judge, will award to me on that day – and not only to me, but also to all who have longed for his appearing."* Paul had not yet received his crown, but it was something he knew awaited him. He had not finished his race, but he could see the finish line.

I thought about going to Addi's gymnastic meets. She had been practicing for months and now the time had come for her to be judged on what she had learned. Everyone's eyes were glued to the score board to see how the judges voted. Addi did not win that day, but she did her best. I have learned life is not about winning, but it is about doing your best and finishing well.

I am renewed because my efforts are not in the hands of men, but in the hands of the "Righteous Judge". The one who knows me and does not compare me to other's abilities or gifts, but awards me or what I am able to do based on what He has given just to me. I don't have to be in competition with anyone else to win. I love the latter part of this verse because Paul's reward is a shared reward for all those on the same team. It's called the "Team Trophy". Everyone shares in the victory. No one is left out, no one is better than anyone else.

Together we are winners. Apart or separate we are nothing.

1 Corinthians 12:21-26 says, *"The eye cannot say to the hand, 'I don't need you!' And the head cannot say to the feet, 'I don't need you!' On the contrary, those parts of the body that seem to be weaker are indispensable, and the parts that we think are less honorable we treat with special honor. And the parts that are unpresentable are treated with special modesty, while our presentable parts need no special treatment. But God has put the body together, giving greater honor to the parts that lacked it, so that there should be no division in the body, but that its parts should have equal concern for each other. If one part suffers, every part suffers with it; if one part is honored every part rejoices with it."*

Love you,

Mom

"Seizing Opportunities"

Good Morning Children,

In Bible Study we have been studying 2 Timothy and today we studied 4:16-18. Paul was in prison and about to be killed for his teachings. Most of us think that if we do or live just the right way to please God, then we will not have any troubles or have to suffer. In some ways we think we will or should receive great rewards. Well this was not the case in Paul's life. He had sacrificed everything he had, including his own life to proclaim the message of God. This passage helped me this morning to look at anything that happens to us as an opportunity to advance the kingdom.

Verse 16 says, *"At my first defense, no one came to my support, but everyone deserted me."* The courtroom is full, and the streets are filled to overflowing. The judge is behind the desk, and the prosecuting attorney is present. The officials bring Paul into the room in chains, but no one is there supporting Paul. No one on his defense team, no witnesses. Everyone has deserted him. Instead of being mad, he prays for his friends. He knows how hard it is for them. For them to stand up and speak for him would mean death for them as well, and yet he prays, *"May it not be held against them"* (Verse 16).

Verse 17 goes on to say, *"But the Lord stood at my side and gave me strength, so that through me the message might be fully proclaimed and all the Gentiles might hear it."* Paul knew he was not completely alone. He knew that wherever he was and whatever was happening to him that God was there giving him strength. What an opportunity they had together! God had placed Paul in just the right place to get the attention of all those people to proclaim His name. Paul did not see it as a setback, but as a comeback! It was not about Paul, it was about the Kingdom. This is so important to remember because we are told in His word that we are never alone, that He will never forsake us and yet this does not mean we will not suffer or go through hard times. God has a purpose for our lives; not to bring us glory, but to bring Him glory.

The second part of this verse continues, *"And I was delivered from the lion's mouth."* You may look at this and say he didn't deliver Paul because he was about to be killed. Again it is not about Paul's safety because if that were true he would not have endured beating, stoning, prison or abandonment. 1 Peter 5:8-9 says, *"Be alert and of sober mind. Your enemy the devil prowls around like a roaring lion looking for someone to devour. Resist him, standing firm in the faith..."* That day Paul *was* delivered from the lion's mouth. The devil did not win.

"The Lord will rescue me from every evil attack and will bring me safely to his heavenly kingdom. To him be glory for ever and ever. Amen." (Verse 18) Paul knew safety was only found in the perfect will of God. He said in Philippians 1:21, *"For to me, to live is Christ and to die is gain."* It's not about this life Kids. In this life you will have troubles of many kinds, but the Lord says He will be with you through them all. Everything that happens to us, He is there. Sometimes we pray for God to deliver us from our circumstances, but I wonder what would have happened if Paul's friends would have bailed him out. I know that all those people would not have heard the message that day.

When Jesus himself was facing death in John 12:27-28 he said, *"Now my soul is troubled, and what shall I say? 'Father, save me from this hour'? No, it was for this very reason I came to this hour. Father, glorify your name!"* Therefore, Kids, whatever happens to us we can give thanks because if God owns us He will use us to bring others to know Him. We are called to make His name known. We are witnesses. What an awesome opportunity we have each day. To God be the glory forever and ever! Amen.

Opportunities await us today. Colossians 4:5 tells us, *"Be wise in the way you act toward outsiders; make the most of every opportunity."*

Love you all,

Mom

"Captivating"

Good Morning Children,

We just returned from Florida. We had a great time and the weather was great! This was an especially great trip for me because Josh and Kelsey were there. I enjoyed watching them so much. Sounds strange, huh? Well, maybe to you, but in a mother's heart are many things. When you have a child, a mother always thinks, *"I wonder who they will marry?"* Over the years I have prayed for your husbands and wives and I did this long before you were even able to date. I remember one day when Bev was really little, I was praying for her husband. She said, *"Mommy, I don't have no husband."* *"Well someday you will Bev, and I want God to watch over him."* In all my dreams I don't think your dad and I could have prayed for a man that loves Bev and their children more than Jon.

Anyway, I was watching Josh as he loved Kelsey. He was kind, considerate and very helpful to her. As she shopped for shoes, he was right there to tell her how nice they looked and helped her look for more. What kind of man does that? Only a man in love. I noticed how he would speak to her with respect, how he would touch her and hold her hand. How he was excited to do the things that interested her. Even when she lost her cell phone, he didn't make any smart remark or degrade her; instead he was concerned for her.

I really loved watching Kelsey love Josh. She sought to serve him every day. I noticed how Kelsey would laugh at Josh's humor. All week she spoke highly of him and how proud she was of him. I noticed her gentle touch to him, even rubbing his stinky feet. As Kelsey and I shared together I knew she had it in her heart to be the best she could be for Josh. All week she was reading material that would prepare her for her marriage. I have heard it said, *"A man should marry the woman he wants to be the mother of his children."* If that is true then Josh picked a winner! Kelsey is wonderful with children and I know she will raise their children with great love and care.

Yes, it was a wonderful trip and my heart is full of praise to God. Kelsey Marie Gray...welcome! You are an amazing woman and thank you for loving Josh. Joshua Douglas...I'm proud of the man you've become and I am so happy for you.

Captivated by His love!

Mom

"I will be glad and rejoice in your love" (Psalms 31:7).

Josh and Kelsey

"Marriage"

Good Morning Children,

Tomorrow Dad and I will celebrate 35 years of marriage. As I have been reflecting, I thought it would be good to share my thoughts on what your dad has done for me.

I have been reflecting on Ephesians 5:25-27. Verse 25 starts, *"Husbands, love your wives, just as Christ loved the church and gave himself up for her."* Often I hear people who say they love things like, *"I love Ice cream"*, or *"I love a good book"* or *"I love golf"*…etc. These are all things that make them feel good. It is something they might do to satisfy themselves. In this passage, love is spoken of as something you do for someone else. It is a sacrificial love for the betterment of someone else. A husband does not love his wife because she deserves to be loved. He loves his wife to show her how great God's love is, for true love can only be measured by sacrifice. Christ's sacrifice on the cross was a terrible death that God used to restore mankind. In the same way, God chose to use husbands to restore their wives to wholeness. But why did God choose husbands to love this way?

Verse 26 tells us that love is, *"to make her holy."* God's plan for a husband was to use him as a vessel where God could express his sacrificial love to restore his wife to wholeness. As I read this I think of how your dad's love has made me whole. When your dad married me, he married my history and my family as well. A lot of hurts, abuse, and betrayal were inside of me and I did not trust love. Love that is hurt challenges. It has its guard up. But God choose to flow through your dad to be the healing agent in my life. He applied sacrificial love to my wounds just as Christ did for the church. When I was stubborn he would say, *"Come here, you need a hug."* When I was defiant, he would bow down and take responsibility for my actions. He has been Jesus to me in so many ways. Over the years that love has taught me how to love and receive love.

The rest of verse 26 continues, *"...cleansing her by the washing with water through the word."* Life is like a sink. Over time it fills up with a lot of junk and starts getting backed up and begins to overflow. A plumber knows how to fix the traps that cause the water not to flow. He carefully takes his wrench and releases the pressure and begins to clean and wash away all the junk inside and before long water is flowing freely again. Your dad is my plumber!

The process your dad used to clean me out and give me a good washing came through the times he would take God's word and read it over me. Although your dad is an amazing fix it man, he recognized there were some things only God could fix. One of the greatest ways your dad expressed his love to me was during those times of reading God's word over me. It was during those times that God's word cleansed me and healed me. I would think about the passages he would read. They renewed my mind over and over.

Verse 27 says, *"...and to present her to himself as a radiant church, without stain or wrinkle or any other blemish, but holy and blameless."* Me...I'm Dad's offering to the Lord. Dad has been speaking a lot lately about the restoring of God's image on the earth by helping people understand the enemy has been stealing from them, making God's church look like beggars. God wants a holy church, a radiant church without the stains, wrinkles, and blemishes so His glory can be seen on the earth. I thank God for your dad and his leadership over me and our family.

When Dad and I were first married he would tell me that, *"Nothing is better for thee than me."* That has proven to be true! Thirty-five years of marriage and we have weathered the storms and joys of life. I give

God the glory because without Him in our lives I don't know where we would be.

Happy Anniversary Day!

I love you!

Mom

Doug and Sandy's wedding picture

"*Hiding Place*"

Good Morning Children,

> *"You are my hiding place; you will protect me from trouble*
> *and surround me with songs of deliverance."*
> Psalm 32:7

This was my reading for today and I found it very interesting because last night I was lying in bed reading His word and one of the things I told the Lord was, *"You are my hiding place."* I did this because I am very thankful to God and I was reflecting on how far I have come by His love, grace and goodness. When I was a child, my hiding place was my closet. When things would get loud in my house it was a place of refuge for me. Even though I could still hear all the sounds, having the door shut seemed to shield me from what was happening on the other side.

God is a place where we can go anytime and for anything. *"Your life is now hidden with Christ in God"* (Colossians 3:3). You are never alone. When the world gets loud and has its demands on you, He is there in spite of all the sounds that you are still hearing. His word is a shield that protects us no matter what is happening on the other side. *"The Lord is my strength and my shield; my heart trusts in him, and he helps me. My heart leaps for joy, and with my song I praise him"* (Psalm 28:7).

As you go to work today and face the world and all the challenges life may bring. I want to encourage you that there is a hiding place in God. Praying for each of you today.

I love you,

Mom

"Resolving Conflict"

Good Morning Children,

I tried to read this morning and my mind wandered. I tried to pray, but situations that had taken place in my life recently kept coming to mind. The Lord was showing me once again areas I need to work on in me. I did not feel condemned, but sad because I dislike who I am at times. The things I do and the things that come out of my mouth shock me and serve to show me how much I need God's help in my life. I feel like Paul when he said in Romans 7:15, *"I do not understand what I do. For what I want to do I do not do, but what I hate I do."*

Often when times of conflict come into our lives we are quick to look at the other person instead of ourselves. It becomes a battle of who is right or wrong. Control is a good word and so is blame. Conflict in our lives can really show us who we are. Having a relationship with God is more than just Bible reading or prayer. It involves talking and listening about the things in life we deal with. It involves asking questions like *"What just happened?"*, *"Why did I react that way?"*, *"What should I do?"*, or *"What would be honoring to you, God?"* It also involves listening. This is when we can hear what we did, what happened and how it can help us. Lastly it involves confession. *"I need your help Lord! I see how I dishonored your name. Forgive me and help me to forgive others as you have forgiven me."*

Resolving conflict always begins with the Lord. I don't think any of us have the ability to lay down our rights or what we think are our rights. It involves humbling ourselves, going and asking for forgiveness in spite of whether you think you are right or wrong. It involves acknowledging how you have hurt and dishonored another. He gives us both the strength and desire to put others before ourselves.

Kids, the Lord has given me a phrase that has helped me recently. Whenever we cease to love and respect others we always have an increase in loving ourselves.

"...those who hope in the Lord will renew their strength. They will soar on wings like eagles; they will run and not grow weary, they will walk and not be faint" (Isaiah 40:31).

Love you all,

Mom

"Character"

Good Morning Children,

When Dad and I started redoing the house, one of the first things Dad did was secure the foundation because no matter what we would have done to the outside it wouldn't have lasted long. Character is a lot like the foundation of a house because a person's character is as strong as its foundation. It is who we are under the surface. I was reading Psalm 36 this morning where David spoke of the character of those who do not fear the Lord. Some of the characteristics of these people were…

1. *"There is no fear of God before their eyes"* (Verse 1). They do not care what they do. They only want what their eyes see.
2. *"In their own eyes they flatter themselves too much to detect or hate their sin"* (Verse 2). Those who are living in sin have to build themselves up in order to make themselves look good in their own eyes and in the eyes of others. They seek to justify themselves.
3. *"The words of their mouths are wicked and deceitful…"* (Verse 3). They speak lies and lead others astray.
4. *"…they fail to act wisely or do good"* (Verse 3). This is a man who once did good and was wise.
5. *"Even on their beds they plot evil; they commit themselves to a sinful course…"* (Verse 4). In the morning as he rises and as he goes to bed, his feet are on a course of destruction.
6. *"…and do not reject what is wrong"* (Verse 3). He does what is pleasing to him.

The best definition of character is doing what is right when no one else is looking. I try to remind myself that God is the one who sees me. He knows me and my thoughts. The rest of the chapter in Psalms talks about His unfailing love to us as we seek to know Him and His ways. David talks of God's love...

"Your love, Lord, reaches to the heavens,
your faithfulness to the skies.
Your righteousness is like the highest mountains,
your justice like the great deep.
You, Lord, preserve both people and animals.
How priceless is your unfailing love, O God!
People take refuge in the shadow of your wings."
Psalm 36:5-7

In Him is where the character of God can be formed. He is the foundation of all those who trust in Him.

My prayer today is that all of us will allow God to build a solid foundation that in every way He will be honored through our lives.

Watch your thoughts, for they become words.
Watch your words, for they become actions.
Watch your actions, for they become habits.
Watch your habits, for they become your character.
Watch your character, for it becomes your destiny.

Love you,

Mom

"Desire"

Good Morning Children,

I went for a walk this morning after the rain. The rays of sun coming through the clouds were absolutely breathtaking. I talked to the Lord about the desires of my heart. They sounded different today as they were not about the things I wanted or desired, but more about the desire to have a heart that would give Him satisfaction and bring Him joy.

In 1 Chronicles 29:10-20, David prays a prayer to God and says, *"... keep these desires and thoughts in the hearts of your people forever, and keep their hearts loyal to you"* (Verse 18). So what is this *desire* I asked myself? I backed up and read what David had told his people.

It began with praise to the Lord, declaring His greatness, power, glory, majesty and splendor. Declaring everything in heaven and earth belongs to God. His kingdom reigns and is exalted as head over all. Wealth and honor all comes from God for He is ruler of all things. My strength comes from God. Thanksgiving and praise are to His name. Everything I have comes from you and can only offer what you have given us already. It comes from your hand, and all of it belongs to you. You test the hearts of men and are pleased with integrity. Pleased with a willing heart. They end with praise. They all praised the Lord and bowed low and fell prostrate before the Lord.

It left me feeling that whatever I desire here on earth is nothing compared to the desire to know and praise God.

Lots of love and thanksgiving this morning,

Mom

"Inadequacy"

Good Morning Children,

There has been a lot of times in my life when I have felt an overwhelming sense of being inadequate for what I am asked to do or expected to do. My fear is that I just don't have what it takes. I fear that I will fail. The bad thing about that fear is that it will keep me from ever trying and, in God's eyes, ever obeying. Fear is what we are left with when faith is gone. A few weeks ago I was reading Jeremiah. He struggled with feelings of inadequacy. God came to him as a young man and told him He was going to appoint him as His spokesman. Jeremiah looked at all the reasons that he couldn't do this job. Let's look closer at Jeremiah 1:6-9.

"Alas, Sovereign Lord,' I said, 'I do not know how to speak; I am too young.' (Does age or inexperience disqualify us from doing God's work?) *But the Lord said to me, 'Do not say, 'I am too young.' You must go to everyone I send you to and say whatever I command you. Do not be afraid of them, for I am with you and will rescue you,' declares the Lord. Then the Lord reached out his hand and touched my mouth and said to me, 'I have put my words in your mouth.'"* (He equips and sustains those He calls.)

As I thought about this story, I was reminded that my inadequacies are often birthed out of my own inabilities instead of relying on His abilities in my life. It is Him who gives me the strength and touches my life. Feeling inadequate is a good thing, it keeps us humble. It protects us from the pride that says, *"I have what it takes. I don't need help."*

Bottom line, Kids, is we are nothing without Him. I encourage you today if you are feeling inadequate in any area of your life, to first thank God for your shortcomings and then seek Him. For in Him we can do all things according to His will. The battle is His, He is our strength!

Love you so much,

Mom

"Ruined"

Good Morning Children,

One of the words for this age seems to be "ruined". The news this morning is full of images of homes, businesses, bridges, and streets all ruined by the hurricane that just came through. Where do we go from here? Who will come and help us? As a small child I remember living in Cocoa Beach when Hurricane Donna came through. We all had to evacuate. I saw a window blown out of a bakery; and later found out that several people had lost their lives because of that accident. Water was everywhere and the windows in our home had been blown out. It was scary and left me confused.

I was reading this morning about when Isaiah saw the Lord. His response in Isaiah 6:5 was, *"Woe to me!' I cried. 'I am ruined!'"* Life as he once knew it was now going to be different. Things that seem to be important no longer were. Isaiah's priorities changed. He heard the voice of the Lord in verse 8 say, *"Whom shall I send? And who will go for us?"* Jeremiah responded, *"Here am I. Send me!"*

Once a life has seen the Lord, it ought to be ruined. We begin to see His face in the hurting, the injustice, the poor, the dying, and our lives will never be the same again. We are ruined! We are compelled to go into our own streets, the highways, and around the world. We are called to help in times of trouble.

I would like to say this morning, that true life can only be found in Him. Troubles will surely come, but if God is the focus of our lives, we will not see destruction as an end, but as a beginning that can bring hope and healing. I still think the same call is going out from the Lord today. *"Who will go for me?"* Leave your comfort and enter into the life of ruins wherever it may be. *"Here **I** am Lord, send me!"* God does not exist for us, we exist for Him.

I miss and love you all every day!

Mom

"Sponsorship...What It Means"

Good Morning Children,

This last trip to Africa was very exciting for me in regards to the issue of sponsored children. It once again showed me how important it is to be in relationship with your child.

Before we left, Dad had several pictures of kids that needed to be sponsored and presented them to our group. Five of them were sponsored right then. I recall looking at a photo of a little girl named Esther with my friend Lisa. Both of us saw how beautiful this girl was. She had lost both of her parents and was living with her grandmother. Lisa knew this would become her daughter.

On one of the first days at the drop in center, Mike, a pastor, pulled up in his car with Esther. I wish I could express the joy on Esther and Lisa's faces. It was a look of pure joy! A picture that we both had looked at in my kitchen had now come to life. The only thing I can relate it to is the opportunity our family has had of viewing a 4D sonogram of Joselyn; Josh and Kelsey's baby. It is snapshot of what we all are anticipating in March when we can finally see her face!

Before we left for Africa, your Uncle Mark came by to give me a check for a year's support for the child he sponsors. Horizon had chosen a young man named Adolphas for Mark to sponsor because he had lost his previous sponsor. I got to meet him while we were there. He is 17 years old and has one more year of school. What a wonderful young

151

boy! He spent the day with us and I had plenty of time to talk to him. He said he was so thankful to Mark and his wife because now, in his words, *"He could dream again."* He hoped someday to meet them. Marlo, John, and Gary, who were on our team, also met their children. It was a wonderful time. One of the African pastors said, *"One of the heights of joy in an orphan's life is to meet their sponsor. It constitutes the highest honor you can give a child."*

Thank you Kids for your support of these children. I encourage you, even though you cannot always go, do not to forget to write. Sponsorship...what does it mean? Well I'll let God answer that one in James 1:27, *"Religion that God our Father accepts as pure and faultless is this:* (what matters most to God) *to look after* (some say to care for, or to visit) *orphans and widows in their distress and to keep oneself from being polluted by the world."*

Sponsorship means the world to our faith.

Love ya,

Mom

"Time"

Good Morning Children,

A brother went to visit his sister who was sick. When he arrived he immediately got busy doing things around the house. His sister said, *"Come here and just sit down."* "I will soon," he replied. *"I want to finish fixing these cabinets."* Some time had passed and she called out to him again, *"I'd like to talk to you about something."* Fearing what she might say and having to face his fears of her sickness, he replied again, *"I need to fix dinner, it's getting late. We'll talk soon."* He knew he had no intention of having a deep conversation with her. Thoughts filled his mind…*"What would I say? What if I cry?"* From her bed, she said, *"I wish you had a dime for every excuse you make."* He looked down and there laid a dime on the floor.

Believe it or not, just before I awoke this morning I had this vivid story in my mind. As soon as the dime appeared, I woke up. I laid there for some time thinking about it, wondering if it had any meaning for me. I thought of my friend Donna. She has cancer in both lungs and does not have long to live. I did go to see her, it was short, but I said I would come back. I am busy, but part of me doesn't know what I would talk about. I think the point is that I need to go and just sit and hold her hand, and listen to what she has to say.

But what about the dime thing? What's that all about? Perhaps it is the closest thing that rhymes with dime. Time. Whatever it was about, I know one thing. I'm going to go to Donna's and just be there; to give her the gift of my time. So it was a good thing and a reminder to do the things that are most important in our busy lives.

"Religion that God our Father accepts as pure and faultless is this: to look after orphans and widows in their distress and to keep oneself from being polluted by the world" (James 1:27).

Love you all,

Mom

"Buster"

Good Morning Children,

Do you remember Buster? He was a homeless man who had been sleeping under the bridge in town that came to New Life. Your dad fixed him a place to live in the basement of the church. I just loved watching how love and kindness transformed his life. Actually I admired your dad's love and respect for the poor. His approach was to give value to life, so he told Buster he needed someone to watch over the church and to help keep it clean. So he asked Buster to live there. I saw such a change in his life. As I recall Buster never missed church and was faithful to do whatever he was asked. His worship and praise on Sunday morning was something I admired. I knew it was sincere. He loved your dad and would do anything for him, for love has the power to change a life.

Dad and I were thinking about the Buster's of life this morning. Simplicity came to mind. Sometimes we get so caught up in how to reach people that we forget how to love them. Jesus said in 1 Corinthians 13:13-14:1, *"And now these three remain: faith, hope and love. But the greatest of these is love. Follow the way of love…"*

Love much,

Mom

"Embrace the Wilderness"

Good Morning Children,

I had a conversation with Jason last night about *"embracing the wilderness"*. Being in the wilderness means you may not always understand why you're there, or how long you'll be there. Being in the wilderness causes us to wonder at times where God is, what He's doing, or even if He's there.

John the Baptist wondered these things as well I am sure. While he was in prison, he sent some men to Jesus to ask this question in Matthew 11:3, *"Are you the one who was to come, or should we expect someone else?"* Now, here was a man who had prepared the way for Jesus. He knew Him from the womb and yet he questioned Him during one of the toughest times in his life. Jesus answered John's question by sharing all he was doing to bring about the kingdom of God, but he didn't say he would change John's circumstances. Jesus did say of John that no one born of God was greater than him.

I believe one of the greatest learning times in our lives is in the wilderness, during that time we seek God and learn from Him. It is also a time of discovery and preparation for what is to come.

Jason, I thank God for where you are and I know He is teaching, directing, and preparing your life for service to Him. Kids, we all go through wilderness times in our lives. My greatest growth in Christ was during those times. So embrace the wilderness.

"In the wilderness prepare the way for the Lord; make straight in the desert a highway for our God" (Isaiah 40:3).

Love to all,

Mom

"The Closet"

Good Morning Children,

Many times as I pass the closet in the hallway I think of Addi, Brody and Ayla. I can hear the giggles, screams and slamming of that door. They call…*"You can't find us!"* To which I respond, *"Where are you? I wonder where those kids are?"* I rattle the door just to hear the squeals, and then I quickly open it and they all scream!

Something about hide and seek is so much fun. Perhaps they love the attention, the discovery, the surprise, or maybe it's the challenge of seeing how long it takes for me to find them.

I started thinking about how we play hide and seek from God at times. We think we are hiding, but He always knows where we are. He is always seeking us out just to have fun with us. Sometimes I think God is hiding from me when I cannot seem to find Him. I seek to find Him and His will for my life. Perhaps He just allows us to hide in the closet just long enough to start calling out His name…*"God! Come find me!"* One thing for sure is He's always close to us.

"If you seek him, he will be found by you" (1 Chronicles 28:9).

Love you,

Mom

"What Are the Things We Love?"

Good Morning Children,

Before I left for Florida, I was talking with Jose. Jose said to me, *"Americans are so different. They love lots of things. They love ice cream, clothes, shoes, houses."* So I asked him, *"So what are the things you love?"* *"I no love things,"* He replied in his broken English. *"I love my son and I love you. Americans have no time for people, only things. They no work for to help people. They work for things,"* he replied.

I thought a lot about what he said. I began to randomly ask people what they loved. To my surprise most people responded by saying things like, *"I love the beach. I love a good book. I love my job. I love fishing. I love a good movie…etc."*

When I got to Florida I asked Ayla, my three year old granddaughter, the same question. She replied, *"I love Mommy and Daddy. I love Papa and you, Nana, I love Addi, Benji, Lexie and Lilly, Jasmin, Mr. Hector and Mrs. Mary."* *"How do you love them?"* I prodded further. *"I hug them, squeeze them, and kiss them. I say I'm gonna get you, and play with them. I tell them I love them,"* she proudly told me. Ayla got the answer right.

Kids, what are the things you love? It's a question I have been asking myself. Matthew 6:21 tells us, *"For where my treasure is, there is my heart also."* Me? You ask. What do I love? I love God. I love your Dad. I love my kids. I love my grandkids. I love my parents and Mary. I love Brody. I love my family and friends. My list could go on and on. The real question is, *"How do I show how much I love and value these people? Who and what do I give my time to?"*

You are my treasures. I love you very much and each day I think of you and pray for each of you. May I find new ways of expressing my love to each of you.

Mom

"Do no love the world or anything in the world. If anyone loves the world, love for the Father is not in them. For everything in the world – the lust of the flesh, the lust of the eyes, and the pride of life – comes not from the Father but from the world. The world and its desires pass away, but whoever does the will of God lives forever" (1 John 2:15-17).

Grandkids

"Come Now"

Good Morning Children,

This morning I woke up and guess what? It was snowing! It may be strange, but I think it is so beautiful. I started thinking about the scripture in Isaiah 1:18. *"'Come now, let us settle the matter,' says the Lord. 'Though your sins are like scarlet, they shall be as white as snow; though they are red as crimson, they shall be like wool.'"* I love that God wants to talk to me about my sins instead of condemning me. The sins He is talking about here are the deep color of scarlet red, which tells me I am deeply coated by the effects of sin. Yet even though I am a sinner, He is able to wash me as white as snow. I am made clean, and no longer stained!

God is a gentle God, overflowing in love and compassion. He is waiting and wanting to talk with us. So often our past hinders us from coming to God. We think we don't measure up or we have failed too much and too often to come to Him. The fact is we will never be perfect, but coming to Him regularly empowers us to live a life in relationship to Him. And it is that relationship that gives us power to overcome sin. It is only by God's grace we are made clean through the blood of Jesus. So, today I remind you of His invitation to "come now". He is ready to listen anytime.

I love you,

Mom

I have begun a study on the names of God and Jesus. I have done this because I want to identify more of who He is; His nature and character. I figure, I have many names: Sandy, wife, daughter, Mom, Nana, sister, aunt, cousin, boss and friend. Each has a different meaning. God has many different roles in our lives, so for the next week I'd like to look at it together.

"Advocate"

Good Morning Children,

"My dear children, I write this to you so that you will not sin. But if anybody does sin, we have an advocate with Father – Jesus Christ, the Righteous One. He is the atoning sacrifice for our sins, and not only for ours but also for the sins of the whole world" (1 John 2:1-2).

The word advocate in Greek means, *"one who is called alongside: an intercessor, a defender."* It is wonderful to know that when I do sin, Jesus is pleading my case before the Father. He is my go-between. The apostle John was writing these words so that I would not sin. When I recognize how much Christ has done for me it causes me to want to do my best, yet the fact is I still fail at times. It is in those times, I know I can count on Jesus to be there for me and forgive the wrong I have done. It is not a cheap grace Kids. The blood of Jesus was a costly sacrifice. It is because of that sacrifice I can become clean. His blood covers my sins. Jesus stands before God, pleading my case as my defense lawyer. I am guilty, yet he paid the price. We are not to be deceived by sin because even though we are forgiven, sin still has consequences. For example if I commit murder, God will forgive me, but I still have to suffer the consequences of my sin, which may be prison.

"Christians are not sinless. But they should sin less."

Advocate! I love it! Thank you Lord for being the one who is always fighting in my defense right alongside of me.

I love you all so much,

Mom

"Jesus the Mediator"

Good Morning Children,

"For there is one God and one mediator between God and mankind, the man Christ Jesus, who gave himself as a ransom for all people" (1 Timothy 2:5-6).

When I think of a mediator, I think of the middle man. It is someone who reconciles two parties at odds with each other, or a peacemaker. In the case of Christ and us, He stepped between God and us and reconciled our relationship. The cost to do this was expensive. He gave His life and died a terrible death. He paid the ransom for you and me. Why would He do this?

Because that is how much He loves us and wants us to be in a right relationship with God. The only way we are acceptable to God is through Christ. As much as I love you and would give my life for you, I could not be the one who makes your relationship with God acceptable. Only Christ has the power to do that. When God looks at us, He sees us through His son Jesus. He is our only go-between. I thank God for the sacrifice Jesus paid.

I love you,

Mom

"Who's Your Daddy?"

Good Morning Children,

On Monday's I have the joy of watching Norah. We have gone out each week and had lunch with friends. Wherever I take her, people always say things like, *"I know whose baby she is. She looks just like her daddy!"*

Jesus was teaching his disciples about God's image in Him. I have been reading John 14:5-14. In verses 7-10 Jesus says,

"'If you really know me, you will know my Father as well. From now on, you do know him and have seen him.' Philip said, 'Lord, show us the Father and that will be enough for us.' Jesus answered, 'Don't you know me, Philip, even after I have been among you such a long time? Anyone who has seen me has seen the Father. How can you say, 'Show us the Father?' Don't you believe that I am in the Father, and that the Father is in me? The words I say to you I do not speak on my own authority. Rather, it is the Father, living in me, who is doing his work."

This morning I keep thinking that even though we may look like our earthly fathers or mothers, how do we reflect our heavenly father? How am I known? Is God's name known through me? Do people say, *"Hey, I know who you belong to."* or *"I see God in you."*?

Just this week, Dad and I were having dinner with K Paul. He said he had spoken to a group of people and had used an illustration of God's love being shown through a 7 year old girl. He said he was so impressed watching this little girl because she was never told what to do. She was so engaged in ministry, serving young and old. Her life reflected God's nature and you knew who she belonged to. He also acknowledged her parents for living a life of service which made it natural when it came to serving. The little girl was Addi.

My prayer today is that each of us would live our lives in such a way that others say, *"You look just like your Father God!"*

Love you all,

Mom

Sandy and Daddy

"Smile"

Good Morning Children,

What is it that makes you smile? Stop and think a minute. Ok, did even the thought bring a smile to your face?

This week a young father came into the café carrying his little daughter. We were talking and I asked him what he liked best about being a father. He replied as a smile covered his face, *"She makes me smile. I love to watch her stretch and her smile at me each morning."*

I thought about what makes me smile. The first thing that came to mind was getting off a plane, walking towards baggage and all of the sudden I hear that wonderful word…Nana! My heart races and I get the biggest smile. Hey, even now just the thought of it makes me smile. I thought of how Josh makes me smile when he does funny things like chasing after the kids. Joy fills my heart as I hear Bev sing or Dad playing the drums. I think of how much I smiled at each game I went to see Chris play. Jason? Well, I smile at the fact that the young father that came into the café that day was him. I smile watching him care for Norah. I smile each day as Brody gives me a morning hug. I smile at all the wonderful pictures Tammy takes that are truly amazing! I smile when I think of the compassion Kelsey has for others. I smile when I think of Jon and what a wonderful father he is and how much fun they all have when he is playing with his children in the pool.

As I look in the mirror I can tell that I have smiled a lot for I now have the lines to prove it. What is it that makes God smile? I think it is His children walking in the light of His love, being expressed through loving and smiling at others.

Proverbs 15:13 says, *"A happy heart makes the face cheerful..."*

Thank you all for the smiles.

I love you,

Mom

Joselyn

"The Kingdom of Heaven"

Good Morning Children,

Jesus says in Matthew 19:14, *"Let the little children come to me, and do not hinder them, for the kingdom of heaven belongs to such as these."* Today this scripture spoke something to me in a way it never had before. I was thinking about Norah and what belongs to her. Jesus says it is the Kingdom of heaven. Then I thought…wow! Each time I see her I get to see this gift from God shining through her…His Kingdom. I get to see a glimpse of Heaven. For Norah doesn't care what I look like or what I wear, how I sing or what I have. Her smiles, coos, giggles, dependency and trust remind me of the simplicity of the Kingdom of Heaven.

What would happen if we looked at every child as if the kingdom of heaven had come to us? How would we treat them differently? What could we learn from them?

Addi, Brody, Ayla, and Ben have taught me many things about the Kingdom of Heaven. Just ask a child about God and you will notice they don't have to filter through all the junk the world has taught us. Their insight is amazing. As you know Jason and Tammy moved in across the street from where we live. Some mornings I hear my front door open and I work my way downstairs to see Jason holding Norah. I greet them and immediately notice a smile appear across Norah's face. It melts my heart for in that moment the Kingdom of Heaven has come to me. I can see it so clearly. I can touch it. I can hold it. I can kiss it. I can love it. God's Kingdom!

Jesus loves the little children, all the children of the world. Red and yellow, black and white, they are precious in His sight. Jesus loves the little children of the world.

I love you all,

Mom

Norah and Nana

"Where's God"

Good Morning Children,

Growing up I loved to play hide and seek. I still do. It is one of the games Norah and I like to play. I will run and hide and say, *"Where's Nana?"* I can hear her little feet and her giggles as she searches for me. When she finds me, I yell, *"You found me!"* To which she bursts out with laughter.

Have you ever wondered where God is? You've been searching for Him? You know He is there, but you cannot see Him. Is He hiding? Does He care?

I was reading John 14:21, *"Whoever has my commands and keeps them is the one who loves me. The one who loves me will be loved by my Father, and I too will love them and show myself to them."* If you want God to show himself to you; to reveal where He is to you, you must obey the sound of His voice. In order to hear His voice you must know Him and what He sounds like and follow that voice because it will lead you to where God is. Great joy and excitement are awaiting those who find Him.

This morning I would like to encourage you to not only know God's commands, but obey them. Obedience is the greatest way to find God.

Love you,

Mom

"Who is With You?"

Good Morning Children,

Yesterday, I was with Norah and we had a wonderful day. I started thinking about who Jesus said is with me. Mark 14:7 says, *"The poor you will always have with you, and you can help them any time you want. But you will not always have me."* With me?

John 12:8 tells us, *"You will always have the poor among you, but you will not always have me."* Among me? Now let me get this straight. If the poor are always with me, and I am always to have the poor among me, then I have to ask the following questions. Where are they? Do I see them? And are they my circle of friends? Among me?

I know that Jesus is always with me and goes with me throughout my day, but how do I recognize him? Not just with my heart, but with my eyes? How do I include Him into my life each day?

Do you think He is in those in whom He said would always be with me? The poor? I do remember Jesus saying that whatever I do for others who are suffering, such as inviting them to dinner, visiting those who are lonely, or taking someone shopping; then it would be a way to know He is with me and among me.

My thought this morning is whatever I do; I must include the poor in the way I live. To make sure I don't ignore their presence, so that they are not forgotten or unseen. As I work, a portion should be set aside to help. When I eat, I need to make sure others are enjoying food. When I buy clothing, I need to make sure others are warm.

The poor are always with us and among us. Lord give us eyes to see them today.

You are always with me every day! I love you so very much!

Mom

"*Trustworthiness*"

Good Morning Children,

While I was in Nicaragua, I was presented with a need. Yes, there were many, but this one was different. My friend Julia has a sister named Adela. I visited her in the hospital. She was in need of a machine that could help her breathe. She needed $100. I did not have it right then and at the time I did not commit to giving it to her. God had brought it to mind several times and in describing this I will try to be honest about my thought process. I started trying to justify myself on all I had been doing and giving lately. I was thinking I still needed to raise funds for Africa, but after talking to the Lord about it I felt He said, *"This one cannot wait. Give the $100."* Then for some reason, I began reading Luke 16:10-11, *"Whoever can be trusted with very little can also be trusted with much, and whoever is dishonest with very little will also be dishonest with much. So if you have not been trustworthy in handling worldly wealth, who will trust you with true riches?"*

Ouch! Well I sent an email and said I would be sending the money for the machine. It wasn't that I didn't want to give it; it was just that I was thinking of my needs first. I was being selfish. I find it is easy to give when I have as opposed to when I don't. God wants above all else for me to be obedient and trust Him with all that I have and it doesn't just have to be money.

I wrote the following in my journal…

"God is not so concerned about changing my situation as He is about changing my attitude and developing my character. God requires my

178

obedience before my situations change. Will I give to God that which will cost me nothing? God desires to give me more...why? So I can give more. Lord, help me to be more faithful to what you have given to me."

As Paul Harvey would say, *"Here's the rest of my story."* After I had made the commitment to give and sealed it by writing an email, a lady that came to my house that same morning gave me an unexpected check for...you guessed it. $100! She did not know the need and the check was not designated. In fact I didn't even know the check was for $100 until after she left. God already knew the way to provide. It truly made me smile and I am amazed again.

I love you,

Mom

"Remember"

This week we were studying Titus 3:1-2. Paul is reminding us of six things that will help us live in this present age.

"Remind people to be subject to..."

1. **Rulers and authorities** – This group would include our President, local government, parents, husbands, bosses and anyone who has been given a position of authority or rules over certain areas.
2. **To be obedient** – To God and to those in authority.
3. **To be ready to do whatever is good** – To everyone as I have been given the opportunity.
4. **To slander no one** – Not to speak anything that would injure the character of anyone, but to pray for them and not to speak evil of them.
5. **To be peaceable and considerate** – I liked the reminder to be considerate, to value others.
6. **To show true humility towards ALL men** – Humbling ourselves to others with sincere hearts and not with false humility.

It was good to remember the way we treat each other because I know I sometimes forget.

Thank you Lord for the authorities you have established and for those who rule over us. I pray we would all be obedient to your word and ready to do whatever is good. Help us to slander no one, but to be ready to build up. May we be considerate to all people and live a life that is full of peace. Give

180

to us the ability to lay down our lives for the sake of all people and to love with sincere hearts.

I love you Lord and I love you all,

Mom

"Catch Me If You Can"

Good Morning Children,

For the last several months my Bible study has been looking at the book of Titus. This book continually talks about doing good. I decided my morning devotions with the grandkids would be on *"doing good"*. I read Titus 2:11-14, *"For the grace of God has appeared that offers salvation to all people. It teaches us to say "No" to ungodliness and worldly passions, and to live self-controlled, upright and godly lives in this present age, while we wait for the blessed hope – the appearing of the glory of our great God and Savior, Jesus Christ, who gave himself for us to redeem us from all wickedness and to purify for himself a people that are his very own, <u>eager to do what is good</u>."*

So the phrase for the day was *"be eager to do what is good"*. I told them *"eager"* means to be more than ready, but excited to do something for someone else. Each time I asked them to repeat the phrase they all said, *"Be eager to **be** good."* *"No! Be eager is to **DO** good!"* I corrected them and explained further. It is not about being good because that focuses us on ourselves. I explained that doing good focuses on doing good to others and when they are doing good to others they are being good.

At the end of the day I sat them down and said, *"Ok, now I want us to look at how eager we were to do good today."* Ayla was eager to help Addi find her charm. When Brody was struggling to carry a bucket of balls during softball practice, Ayla ran to help. Addi was eager to care for Ben's needs, buckling him in the car and helping him find the toy car he lost at the ball field. Ben was eager to sit with Brody at the ball game and chase Addi's practice balls. It was good at the end of the day to go over these things because none of them even thought about the fact that they were doing good. They just were.

Today the verse I read was Titus 3:1-2, *"Remind the people to be subject to rulers and authorities, to be obedient, to be ready to do whatever is good, to slander no one to be peaceable and considerate, and always to be gentle toward everyone."* The phrase today is *"Be ready to do what is good"*. So this morning I told them about the *"Catch Me If You Can"* game that I wanted to play. I reminded them again not to try to be good, but to do something good for someone else. I told them we need to catch each other *"doing good"* and when they catch someone they have to yell, *"Caught ya!"* Oh my goodness! I could make a list a mile long. They are so eager to get started! Ready, set, GO! Ready to do good, set your mind to do good, and then GO and do good!

Love you all,

Mom

"Be Examples by Doing What Is Good"

Good Morning Children,

"In everything set them an example by doing what is good. In your teaching show integrity, seriousness and soundness of speech that cannot be condemned, so that those who oppose you may be ashamed because they have nothing bad to say about us" (Titus 2:7-8).

We are still having a lot of fun learning about doing what is good. So far we have learned that we should be eager to do good, we should be ready to do good, and to be an example of doing what is good.

The kids were still engaged in playing the *"Caught You"* game. Brody said, *"Look, Nana, I am being an example of Christ by doing good to Ben."* I showed him how to treat others who need help. Wow…he gets it!

People are looking at our lives each day. To be honest, there are days I am a good example and days when my life is not a good example. I need to remind myself that He is the God who knows me and He is looking at me each day.

Love you,

Mom

"Teach What is Good"

Good Morning Children,

"Likewise, teach the older women to be reverent in the way they live, not to be slanderers or addicted to much wine, but to teach what is good" (Titus 2:3).

As you know I have been in Florida with my grandchildren. The phrase for today was *"Teach what is Good"*. Beverly gathered her children and their friends and was teaching them a visual lesson today. She got a candle and explained to them that our lives are like a candle. When it is lit, it gives light to others around us. Then she took all of us to the bathroom and shut the door. She pointed out how much light the candle made in the darkness. Our lives are the exact same. We can give light to those in darkness. Then she took a bowl and covered the light and put out the candle. Darkness was all around us. This showed the kids that if we hide our light, no one can see the light God gives us.

Matthew 5:14-16 tells us, *"You are the light of the world. A town built on a hill cannot be hidden. Neither do people light a lamp and put it under a bowl. Instead they put it on its stand, and it gives light to everyone in the house. In the same way, let your light shine before others, that they may see your good deeds and glorify your Father in heaven."*

I caught you Bev! Teaching what is right!

Love you all,

Mom

"Learn to Devote Yourself to Doing What is Good"

Good Morning Children,

I enjoyed learning from Bev while we were together. I loved learning what God has been teaching her and how she is applying those things in her life and ministry. I find that when we share what we are learning with others we are growing and the people that are listening grow as well. I gained a lot last week!

One of the best things Bev told me was what she learned at a Women of Faith conference she attended. It was about monkeys. There was a test done on a monkey. It was put inside a cage and prompted to do the same things continuously. The stress level of that monkey was very high. They did the test a second time, only this time they put another monkey in the same cage. The stress level of the monkeys was much lower than when they were alone. The point is that we all need monkeys in our lives to hold us when our stress levels get high.

So Kids, learn to devote your selves to do what is good, and find another monkey to do it with!

Love you,

Mom

"Careful to Devote Themselves to Doing What is Good"

Good Morning Children,

In order to understand the text of Titus 3:8, we need to broaden our view and look at the preceding verses 3-7 as well.

> *"At one time we too were foolish, disobedient, deceived and enslaved by all kinds of passions and pleasures. We lived in malice and envy, being hated and hating one another. But when the kindness and love of God our Savior appeared, he saved us, not because of righteous things we had done, but because of his mercy. He saved us through the washing of rebirth and renewal by the Holy Spirit, whom he poured out on us generously through Jesus Christ our Savior, so that, having been justified by his grace, we might become heirs having the hope of eternal life. This is a trustworthy saying. And I want you to stress these things, so that those who have trusted in God may <u>be careful to devote themselves to doing what is good</u>. These things are excellent and profitable for everyone."*

When we realize how much Jesus did for us by giving us His grace and mercy, it causes us to desire to be careful to devote ourselves to Him and do what is good. When you find yourself realizing you have not devoted yourself to doing what is good, remember, His mercies are new each day. Today is a new day filled with so many opportunities to do good.

Let us seize those opportunities and do good and at the same time be careful because in the midst of doing good, evil is there too.

I love you all,

Mom

"Love What is Good"

Good Morning Children,

A quick review...

Be eager to do what is good.
Be ready to do what is good.
Be an example to do what is good.
Teach what is good.
Learn to devote yourself to do what is good.
Be careful to devote yourself to do what is good.
And finally...Love what is good.

1 John 4:16 tells us who love is. *"God is love. Whoever lives in love lives in God, and God in them."* But what is love? 1 Corinthians 13:4-8 says, *"Love is patient, love is kind. It does not envy, it does not boast, it is not proud. It does not dishonor others, it is not self-seeking, it is not easily angered, it keeps no record of wrongs. Love does not delight in evil but rejoices with the truth. It always protects, always trusts, always hopes, always perseveres. Love never fails."* 1 John 4:11 instructs us, *"Dear friends, since God so loved us, we also ought to love one another."*

"And this is love: that we walk in obedience to his commands. As you have heard from the beginning, his command is that you walk in love" (2 John 1:6).

I love you all, but my love is not perfect. I am not always patient or kind. I am selfish and sometimes I envy what I do not have. I am proud and even rude at times. But what my heart desires is to love what is good.

When I realize I am not loving the way God loves, I acknowledge my actions and turn once again to Who love is. My God is able to help me love the way I should. He is my standard of how to love others. When I fail to love correctly I find comfort in 1 John 4:10, *"This is love: not that we loved God, but that he loved us and sent his Son as an atoning sacrifice for our sins."*

He loves us and is committed to us. He forgives us and empowers us to be more and more in love with what is good.

Thankful for His love,

Mom

"Once and for All"

Good Morning Children,

I was studying for Bible Study this morning and we are looking at the seven statements made about Christ in Hebrews 1:2-4. In verse 3, the statement is made, "...*he had provided purification for sins...*" This reminded me of a woman I prayed with for quite some time in Zimbabwe. This woman was crying and weeping over her sins, pleading for God to forgive her. I asked her how long she had been doing this and she had been for years. I asked her if she had turned from her sin, which she had done so years before that. Then I told her that Christ had paid the price and that she needed to just thank Him for the rest of her life and not live as if Christ hadn't done the finished work on the cross. I told her He had already provided forgiveness for her sins and she needed to accept it, and praise God for it! Then I prayed with her to receive God's gift of forgiveness and no longer live in the bondage of the weight that sin had held on her.

Don't we do that as well sometimes? The devil would love nothing more than to hold us captive to our sins or hold captive the sins of others. Jesus came to set us free.

Hebrews 7:26-27 says, "*Such a high priest truly meets our need – one who is holy, blameless, pure, set apart from sinners, exalted above the heavens. Unlike the other high priests, he does not need to offer sacrifices day after day, first for his own sins, and then for the sins of the people. He sacrificed for their sins <u>once and for all</u> when he offered himself.*"

Hebrews 9:12 tells us, *"He did not enter by means of the blood of goats and calves; but he entered the Most Holy Place <u>once and for all</u> by his own blood, thus obtaining eternal redemption."* Verse 14 continues, *"How much more, then, will the blood of Christ, who through the eternal Spirit offered himself unblemished to God, cleansed our consciences from acts that lead to death, so that we may serve the living God!"*

Did you get that last part? God frees us from our sin to be able to serve Him. I know so many people that live in their sin and it causes them to not live in what God is calling them to do.

Kids, if you are living in any way under the bondage of your past sins, I want you to know today that if you have asked for forgiveness and have turned from your ways, Jesus paid the price ONCE AND FOR ALL! Praise be to God! That, in and of itself, will keep our lives free to serve Him with all our hearts in thankfulness.

Walk in love and forgiveness.

Love you all!

Mom

"Christmas Surprise"

Good Morning Children,

Dad and I drove to the beach last night. After we arrived, we got out and began to walk. It was a beautiful night. The moon and stars were shinning, the waves were crashing and the smell of good old salt water filled the air. As we continued to walk I noticed in the distance a beautifully set table nestled in the sand. It had a Christmas green table cloth, complete with roses and what looked like a bottle of wine. A circle of candles surrounded the table with more flowers.

"Wow!" I thought someone went to a lot of trouble to create something special. As we approached a set of stairs that led down to the beach, I heard two familiar voices giggling with excitement. There at the bottom of the stairs were Addi and Ayla. It took me by great surprise. Dressed in their Christmas dresses, they held Christmas red, handmade menus. *"Welcome!"* they yelled. *"Dinner is served. Follow us."*

They led us past a sign that they had written on the sand that said, "Doug and Sandy". There before me was the beautifully set table. John was playing the guitar and Bev was singing. The kids sat us down and began to pour us sparkling cider. As tears filled my eyes, I could see Dad was not surprised. *"What's going on?"* I asked. He took my hand and said, *"I wanted to do something special for you, so I planned this and asked Bev to help me do it. It was Christmas 36 years ago that we walked on the beach and I asked you to be my wife."* He gave me a card and recited a poem he had written and said, *"I wanted to remind you of my love."*

I felt special. Everyone was excited and crying too. Bev had prepared a meal and the girls began to serve us. The entertainment was the songs that the girls sang to us, and after we ate, Bev and Jon sang a special song to which we danced. To complete our evening, Addi led us to what she called the "Circle of Love". It was a heart drawn in the sand. It was a very special evening that we were able to share with our family. I wish you all could have been there.

1 Corinthians 13:4 says, "...*love is kind...*"

This Christmas I would like all of you to know how special you are to Dad and me. We are family and we all love one another. I am so blessed and thankful that 36 years ago I said, "*Yes!*" Merry Christmas, Kids. I love you so much.

Mom

"*Importance*"

Good Morning Children,

When I think of what is most important to me I would say without hesitation it would be my family. I love each of you very much, and what happens in your life matters deeply to me. I was also thinking for the last few days about what I believe is the most important in God's life. I can say without hesitation that God would also say it is His family. He proved His love for His family by sending us his son to die for us. I know you have heard that your entire life, but let's think about it this morning. Would I sacrifice any of you? The thought makes me sick to my stomach. Would I sacrifice myself for you? Yes. But to give you up or allow you to be beaten up, spit on, used or killed. NO! Why then would God do this? Because He loved what He had created. You and me. He had a plan by showing us this great love so that we could be in right relationship with Him.

The plan then was for us to love as we have been loved, to spread this love and make His name known in the earth as it is in heaven. Jesus taught us how to do this by giving His life away. Each day we have an opportunity to love God's family, to lay down our lives, to give our lives away. Yes, even for those who are not very easy to love or to those who use and hurt us. Matthew 5:46 says, *"If you love those who love you, what reward will you get?"*

A few weeks ago, Tammy shared with me that she and Jason had just received the brochure of a young orphan boy that they had requested through Horizon. I was at their house and they had just received his picture and placed it on the refrigerator with excitement. I was excited for them and I knew God was excited as well. They are loving God's family and caring for those who cannot care for themselves. Dad called a few days ago, and he and the team had gone into the bush area to minister to kids. He said his heart broke all over again for the kids who have nothing.

Loving God's family is the way we can say thank you to God for all he has done for us. It is also a way to love God. *"And this is his command: to believe in the name of his Son, Jesus Christ, and to love one another as he commanded us"* (1 John 3:23).

I love you,

Mom

"Be Careful"

Good Morning Children,

I am sure you can remember growing up and hearing me say, *"You better be careful, you're going to fall."* Or *"You better be careful, you're going to get in trouble."* It was always a warning or a word of instruction because I cared about you and could see what you were about to do might cause you harm. The same is true with God. He loves us so much and warns us to be careful.

On Wednesday, I met with a Bible Study group. We have been going through the book of Hebrews. Yesterday the passage was Hebrews 2:1-4. It was the first of five warnings that were given to pay attention to His words. *"We must pay the most careful attention, therefore, to what we have heard, so that we do not drift away."* I love that the writer includes himself three times in this passage as *"we"* because we all can be in danger and can drift away from what we have heard. It wasn't that the Christians were forgetting what they had heard. They knew it, yet they just didn't pay attention or respect how dangerous drifting could be.

The following are notes that I took in our Bible study. I pray they will serve as a reminder to heed the warning of drifting away from what we know…

1. Drifting means we are carried away slowly, without even knowing it, until we wake up and discover how far we are away from being safe.
2. Drifting happens when we become neglectful.

3. The antidote for drifting into deep waters is paying attention, being alert.
4. Failure to pay attention to God's word will lead you into sin. The lifeguard calls out to you first. Then he swims out and rescues you from drowning and brings you back to safe ground. He is like the Holy Spirit who is committed to getting us back on course.
5. Drifting is like being connected by an anchor who is God. The rope becomes loose and gets disconnected and whatever it was securing begins to drift away.
6. Chris came into the cafe and said drifting is not having roots, not being secure.
7. It is good to remember it as three R's. **Recognize** you are drifting. **Repent**, turn back to shore. **Restore**, God is able to get you back, pull you closely to Him so that you will be anchored tightly to Him.

The conclusion of our Bible Study group was to not take God's word for granted; to hold it in high regard. Not to become complacent or distracted by other things, but hold on to His word and never let it go.

Love you,

Mom

"*Love is Kind*"

Good Morning Children,

Mother Teresa once said, *"We can do no great things, only small things with great love."* I thought of this yesterday as I spoke with someone who needs to know they are valued. On the outside they appear to be hard, but on the inside they just need love. This person told me about something my dad did last Christmas. He said, *"Your father gave me a card with a gift inside. I could not believe that he would remember me. Why me? No one gives me a card or a gift. I didn't even know how to respond. I was so overwhelmed."* I asked him if he kept the card. *"Yea!"* he said like I had asked a stupid question. *"It is under my pillow and I look at it every night."* I guess I asked because the last time I received a card from my dad, I threw it away. It made me think of how much I take love for granted. What if I had no one to love me?

I see the same thing when I go to Africa. People appreciate a touch so much more there than here. Why? Because hugs are few and far between there. Love means so much more when you don't have it. Jesus taught us to love even when it is not easy because those who need it the most are those who don't have it.

"If you love those who love you, what credit is that to you? Even sinners love those who love them. And if you do good to those who are good to you, what credit is that to you? Even sinners do that. And if you lend to those from whom you expect repayment, what credit is that to you? Even sinners lend to sinners, expecting to be repaid in full. But love your enemies, do good to them, and lend to them without expecting to get anything back. Then your reward will be great, and you will be children of the Most High, because

he is kind to the ungrateful and wicked. Be merciful, just as your Father is merciful" (Luke 6:32-36).

I am thankful for your love,

Mom

"The God who See's"

Good Morning Children,

I read the story of Hagar, the servant girl of Sarai in Genesis 16. Sarai was not able to give birth to a child. Hagar, her servant, gave birth to a child through Sarai's husband at Sarai's request. She then became jealous and mistreated Hagar until Hagar ran away. Hagar was hurt, misunderstood, taken advantage of, used, and abused. I am sure she felt alone and isolated.

In the midst of Hagar's tears, God appears and Hagar says in verse 13, *"You are the God who sees me..."* You care. You came.

My thought this morning is this. When I was a young mother I was there to fare for you, kiss your boo boo's and wipe away your tears. I am sure at one time Hagar had a mother who did that for her, but now she finds herself alone. Now that you are older, I am sure all of you have felt like Hagar at one time or another. Alone. God is someone who is always there. In verse 13, Hagar also said, *"I have now seen the One who sees me."*

My prayer this morning is that you will always know God is with you. He sees and knows all. I pray that during those times you will see God as well. I love you. Each morning Dad and I pray for you.

Sealed with a kiss from my heart.

Mom...who was once called Mommy

"Open Wide Your Hearts"

Good Morning Children,

When I was growing up, one of the things I remember saying to my brothers, as I opened my arms wide to them was, *"I love you this much!"* It was my way of saying, *"I open my heart to you and watch out because you are about to get a hug!"*

This morning as I was reading in 2 Corinthians 6, Paul told the Corinthians in verses 11-12, *"We have spoken freely to you, Corinthians, and opened wide our hearts to you. We are not withholding our affection from you..."* So often we hold back showing affection or opening wide our hearts in fear that our love will be rejected.

Therefore, our arms are rarely extended and our hearts are closed off. Paul encourages them at the end of verse 13 to, *"...open wide your hearts also."* He refers to this as a fair exchange. But what if love is not fair? I give love and yet I don't seem to receive it? Does our love depend on what we receive or on what we choose to give? The scripture that comes to mind is, *"Give, and it will be given to you"* (Luke 6:38). When we choose to give, especially when it is not fair, we become like Jesus. He gave when it was not fair. He spread His arms wide open as He hung on the cross for love.

I encourage you today, Kids, to open wide your hearts.

Love you so much,

Mom

"Warnings"

Good Morning Children,

This Sunday, Dad and I visited a church that was meeting in a school building. In the middle of the service the fire alarm went off. No one left the building and the pastor even said, *"I am sure there is not a fire. Just stay put."* Most put their hands over their ears because the alarm was loud and piercing. The fire department came and ordered everyone out of the building.

There are inconveniences in life and many interruptions. Sometimes we are just like the people sitting in that school when it comes to God's word. We hear it and know it and yet we do not heed its warnings. We just stay seated. We know we need to obey His warnings to get up and leave, but don't. We don't really believe His warnings are true and have consequences, so we get burned. We tune out the Spirit by putting our hands over our ears and we become deaf to His voice. We even tell ourselves to stay put because things will be fine and the alarms do not apply to us. We become proud.

Then God's love shows up with authority and orders you to get out. He is not concerned about your inconveniences, interruptions or your comforts. He is concerned for your very life. Kids do not minimize God's warnings about life. They are given to us because He loves us so much. They are protections and provisions by a loving, caring Father.

"The law of the Lord is perfect, refreshing the soul. The statutes of the Lord are trustworthy, making wise the simple. The precepts of the Lord are right, giving joy to the heart. The commands of the Lord are radiant, giving light

to the eyes. *The fear of the Lord is pure, enduring forever. The decrees of the Lord are firm, and all of them are righteous. They are more precious than gold, than much pure gold; they are sweeter than honey, than honey from the honeycomb. By them your servant is warned; in keeping them there is great reward"* (Psalms 19:7-11).

My prayer today is Psalm 19:14,*"May these words of my mouth and this meditation of my heart be pleasing in your sight, Lord, my Rock and my Redeemer."*

Love you all,

Mom

"*Learned Obedience*"

Good Morning Children,

I am learning a lot, but learning and applying is somewhat different. God has been teaching me many things and I am learning to hear Him in ways I have not heard Him before. Most of all I am learning to be obedient to the things He is teaching me. I can tell you though it is hard because I must die to myself. I am learning that obedience is the key to life and healing. Being obedient shows that I truly trust God and believe His ways are the only way to life. He leads us down paths that require us to lay down our lives, yet in return it is the only way that leads to life. I have found that it is not until we obey that we reap the joy of what we are struggling with, not before. Just knowing what is right is not enough.

This morning I was reading in Hebrews 5:7, *"During the days of Jesus' life on earth, he offered up prayers and petitions with fervent cries and tears to the one who could save him from death, and he was heard because of his reverent submission."* Although he was a son, he <u>learned obedience</u> from what he suffered. It was not easy even for Jesus. He cried loud cries. He struggled just like we do. The suffering we go through in this life does not compare with who He is. Jesus could go through anything because he loved the Father and could trust Him completely even though it meant death to Himself.

I feel like a caterpillar sometimes. All wrapped up inside a safe little place. *"Don't mess with my space God. I can't handle the stresses of life or the unknown. Just let me stay here where I am comfortable and secure."* No!

God wants us to fly! So, press through the struggle; before you know it, you'll be free.

Love you all,

Mom

"Going On"

Good Morning Children,

I spoke with a person yesterday who was going through a really tough time. In our conversation they said, *"How can I go on?"* I thought of the words of Paul when he was going through really tough times in his life. He says in 2 Corinthians 12:1, *"…I will go on to visions and revelations from the Lord."*

Sometimes going on is hanging on! Hanging on to every word God is speaking to us. Obeying Him even when we don't feel like it. Paul had what He described as, "a thorn in the flesh," something that tormented him. He pleaded with the Lord to take it away. Sound familiar? But here is how the Lord responded to him in verse 9, *"My grace is sufficient for you, for my power is made perfect in weakness."* Paul responded at the end of verse 9 and continued to verse 10, *"Therefore I will boast all the more gladly about my weaknesses, so that Christ's power may rest on me. That is why, for Christ's sake, I delight in weaknesses, in insults, in hardships, in persecutions, in difficulties. For when I am weak, then I am strong."*

How does this work? When we face difficulties we become dependent on Him because, the fact is, we cannot manage by ourselves. But He can. We must surrender; give up our rights to be right and our desire to be in control. When you are facing hardships in life, Kids, when you are too tired to go on, too weak to fight, remember the Lord. He is faithful and will provide us with the answers we need to go on and the strength to do it.

As much as my heart loves each of you, God loves you more.

He is able,

Mom

"Arrogance"

Good Morning Children,

I was reading the story of Nebuchadnezzar this morning. I noticed how arrogant he was and how he thought he controlled everything. He said in Daniel 4:30, *"Is not this the great Babylon I have built as the royal residence, by my mighty power and for the glory of my majesty?"* He had a dream. Daniel interpreted the dream something like this. *"...that tree, Your Majesty, is you. For you have grown strong and great; your greatness reaches up to heaven, and your rule to the ends of the earth. Then you saw God's angel coming down from heaven and saying, 'Cut down the tree and destroy it, but leave the stump and the roots in the earth surrounded by tender grass, banded with a chain of iron and brass"* (Verses 22-23). *"For seven years this will be your life, until you learn that the Most High God dominates the kingdoms of men and gives power to anyone he chooses"* (Verse 25).

The King suffered greatly and in the end he says in verses 34-35, *"...I, Nebuchadnezzar, raised my eyes toward heaven, and my sanity was restored. Then I praised the Most High; I honored and glorified him who lives forever. His dominion and eternal dominion; his kingdom endured from generation to generation. All the peoples of the earth are regarded as nothing. He does as he pleases with the powers of heaven and the peoples of the earth."*

I know most of us like to plan for the future. We have lots of plans, but who determines them? Us? If we believe this, we become delusional like Nebuchadnezzar. Our hearts will fail when our plans do. We complain about what we have and who we are. We rarely ever stop to acknowledge it is God who gave us our very breath and it is He who has given us what we have. When things don't go as we had planned we blame Him and ask Him to change our situation so that it matches our expectations, never considering what He may want to teach us or what He is leading us into.

My encouragement to you today, Kids, is this. God is God and He does as He pleases. The best way to plan for the future is to walk in His ways, acknowledging Him in every step during the good times and the bad. He will use all of them for the good if we choose to trust, submit and obey Him with thanksgiving.

I declare this…He is the Lord Most High, to Him be glory, honor and praise. We are nothing without Him. Our life is not our own, we gave it to Him and we will trust Him with it. He is invisible yet He remains invincible.

There is no one like our God!

Thankful,

Mom

"Choosing"

Good Morning Children,

Several months ago I was thinking about the choices I have in life. I began to make a list of choices that I wanted to make as an offering to God and I prayed I would be able to carry them out each day.

"Now fear the Lord and serve him with all faithfulness. Throw away the gods your ancestors worshiped beyond the Euphrates River and in Egypt, and serve the Lord. But if serving the Lord seems undesirable to you, then choose for yourselves this day whom you will serve, whether the gods your ancestors served beyond the Euphrates, or the gods of the Amorites, in whose land you are living. But as for me and my household, we will serve the Lord" (Joshua 24:14-15).

The first choice I have to make is that of putting God over me. I'm sure you are not shocked that I chose God over Satan? Really, who would ever choose Satan who is a Christian? Yet in reality we choose our ways, which are often influenced by Satan's ways. If God's enemy can get us to serve ourselves he knows this will dishonor God.

My day begins with this choice. Who will I serve? I know it is my desire to serve God with all my heart and yet all throughout my day I am faced with so many choices as to who I will really serve. How many choices do I make which are influenced by my love for God or love of myself? Do my actions or my words testify of who I have chosen? I wish I could say I always choose God but in reality I do not, I sometimes choose myself. I am in this process of living out my choices and my day is filled with many. Paul says of himself in Romans 7:21, *"Although I want to do good, evil is right there with me."*

I am learning that if I position myself to seek God and love Him first by staying in His word and in relationship with Him. I am more aware of what pleases Him and able to make right choices. When I fall short in doing this, I still have the opportunity to make my choices usually by humbling myself, and asking for forgiveness.

I do believe, Kids, that God gives us the ability to say no to ourselves and say yes to God. Titus 2:11-14 says, *"For the grace of God has appeared that offers salvation to all people. It teaches us to say "No" to ungodliness and worldly passions, and to live self-controlled, upright and godly lives in this present age, while we wait for the blessed hope – the appearing of the glory of our great God and Savior, Jesus Christ, who gave himself for us to redeem us from all wickedness and to purify for himself a people that are his very own, eager to do what is good."*

Knowing Jesus gave himself for us, I too want to give Him myself. I want to do what is good and pleasing to Him.

Lord, I pray for my family. I ask your Holy Spirit to empower us to live and act according to your example. I love you all. Dad and I pray for each one of you every morning.

Mom

"Submission Over Rebellion"

Good Morning Children,

According to www.merriam-webster.com, the definition of submission is *"the state of being obedient: the act of accepting the authority or control of someone else"*. When I think of submitting, the first thing that comes to mind is that I am on a mission to submit to an authority higher than myself. Each day I have this burning desire to submit to the will of God. As I read God's word and try to submit to it, I can tell you it is hard, in fact it is impossible to do without Him. What helps me the most is to know that God's ways are the only ways that lead to life for me. I may not always understand them and most of the time I don't. They are so opposite of what I think or feel, but it boils down to trusting God and having faith in Him to know He loves me so much and wants what is best for me.

I can tell you the best thing that has helped me is to have a relationship with the Holy Spirit. Jesus left the Holy Spirit to lead us, guide us, and to be our counselor (John 14:16). He is the one who helps us and gives us power to lay down our lives. The Holy Spirit has caused us to do the impossible in our lives. We take no credit at all because without His help we would not be able to submit or die to our own selfish wants and desires. I don't know if you have ever looked at the Holy Spirit as a person, but I invite you to do that. He is a person. His function is to keep us in the faith; to teach us truth (John 16:5-16). I encourage you to do a study on the Holy Spirit sometime.

Rebellion, according to www.merriam-webster.com, is defined as *"open opposition toward a person or group in authority"*. The ultimate effect of rebellion against God is a hard heart. *"Today, if you hear his voice, do not harden your hearts as you did in the rebellion"* (Hebrews 3:15).

"My son, pay attention to what I say; turn your ear to my words. Do not let them out of your sight, keep them within your heart; for they are life to those who find them and health to one's whole body. Above all else, guard your heart, for everything you do flows from it. Keep your mouth free of perversity; keep corrupt talk far from your lips. Let your eyes look straight ahead; fix your gaze directly before you. Give careful thought to the paths for your feet and be steadfast in all your ways. Do not turn to the right or the left; keep your foot from evil" (Proverbs 4:20-27).

Pray for me today. I will be praying for you!

Mom

"Future vs. Past"

Good Morning Children,

"We find it easy to forget what we should remember and remember what we should forget." – Author Unknown

Philippians 3:13-14 says, *"...Forgetting what is behind and straining toward what is ahead, I press on toward the goal to win the prize for which God has called me heavenward in Christ Jesus."*

To forget something doesn't mean we lose our memory about the events in our life. It means we do not have to live by them. When Paul made this statement he had just finished recalling what he was in the process of forgetting. He had made a conscious decision to go forward. He could not stay behind in what had happened in his life because to do so would have left him defeated and would hinder what God had for him in the future. He even admitted that he wasn't "there" yet. He hadn't arrived. I am sure he had times when he doubted himself and was filled with shame.

He states in verses 10-11, *"I want to know Christ – yes, to know the power of his resurrection and participation in his sufferings, becoming like him in his death, and so, somehow, attaining to the resurrection from the dead."* In order for me to do this I must go forward, I must be in the process of this one thing: "Forgetting." Note that he didn't say he forgot, but that he was in the process of forgetting. I love that he also states he is straining toward the future. Leaving the past is not always easy. The enemy loves to remind us of our failings, but Paul made it his determination to turn towards the future. He could have stayed in the reality of the fact that he hated and murdered hundreds of Christians. But he didn't. I am so glad he moved on because God had a plan to fulfill in his life.

Go forward...God has a wonderful plan for you.

Love you all,

Mom

"Faith vs. Deeds"

Good Morning Children,

It is not only important to know what is right, but to do it. James 2:14-17 says, *"What good is it, my brothers and sisters, if someone claims to have faith but has no deeds? Can such faith save them? Suppose a brother or a sister is without clothes and daily food. If one of you says to them, 'Go in peace; keep warm and well fed,' but does nothing about their physical needs, what good is it? In the same way, faith by itself, if it is not accompanied by action, is dead."*

Selfishness says, *"I want. I have, I will even take and expect others to give to me."* At its root is a lack of trust that God will really take care of me. It causes me to store up for myself and look out for my own needs. James is teaching us that as we meet the needs of others we are showing the genuineness of our faith by how we choose to live our lives. A person of faith is known by what he does, not by what he says he's going to do, or even what he teaches others to do. He must live it out as verse 18 says, *"You have faith; I have deeds. Show me your faith without deeds, and I will show you my faith by my deeds."*

I say these things out of conviction. There are so many times I say to myself, *"I need to go and do this or that..."* Most of it has to do with time for me. I know those who are lonely, depressed, in need and yet I choose to do for myself. "Me" is divided up in so many ways with a little here and a little there. There are needs everywhere, but the question I have to ask myself is, *"What am I doing that God wants and is asking me to do?"* Often I offer up other good things that I choose to do and ask Him to bless them or assume that He will.

Lord, I pray for my family, that all of us would be led by your Spirit. Let us be a people who love in words and actions, so that all may see your love working in us and through us. To you be the glory Lord. Amen.

Love to you all,

Mom

Faith and deeds work together...

"Conflict"

Good Morning Children,

Conflict? It is defined by www.merriam-webster.com as, *"the opposition of persons or forces that gives rise to the dramatic action in a drama or fiction"*.

I suppose we all have had conflicts at one time or another. Some conflicts seem to be constantly before us. It may be at work, at church, at home, or with a neighbor. Conflicts usually are between people. We all have different views of the way things should be and how we should handle them. Most of the time we only see one side and it is usually our own. Sometimes we are hurt and we want to fight back or defend ourselves.

I was reading a few chapters tonight and it spoke to me about conflicts and how to handle them. Are they hard? No. They are impossible, but He tells me in Mark 9:23 that, *"Everything is possible for one who believes."*

I often read God's word as if it were speaking just to me. Tonight it read something like this to me, starting in 1 Peter 3:8 and continuing through chapter 5.

Live in harmony with one another and be sympathetic, loving each other. Be compassionate and humble when someone hurts you. Sandy, do not repay evil for evil, or insult them back, but give blessings instead because of this you were called, so that you would inherit a blessing. Keep a tight rein on your tongue, not speaking evil and keep your lips from speaking lies. Do good, Sandy, and seek peace and pursue it. I am the one who sees you. I am the one who hears your prayers. If you suffer for doing right, you will be blessed. Do not be sucked into fearing what others fear, but be prepared to share the hope that is in you with gentleness and respect. Keep a clear conscience. Be clear-minded and self-controlled so that you can pray effectively.

Love each other deeply and remember that love covers all wrongs. Be hospitable without grumbling. Use the gifts I have placed within you to serve others. Administer God's grace to others in all its various forms. Christ died for everyone's sin, once and for all. If you speak, let your words sound like mine. When you serve do it with the strength you find in me so that in all things God may be praised. Glorify my name. Continue to do good and commit yourself to me. Clothe yourself with humility towards others. Humble yourself under God's hand so that He may lift you up in due time. If you have anxiety about any situation cast them on to me, Sandy, because I want you to know I care for you. I want you to be self-controlled and alert so that you will be able to stand firm against the enemy when he comes. God is a restoring God. His process will make you strong, firm and steadfast. To you, O Lord, be the glory and power forever and ever. Amen!

Love you with all my heart!

Mom

"*Forgiveness*"

Good Morning Children,

Do you have someone in your life that has hurt you? Betrayed you? Spoken falsely against you? I am sure we all have. I would like to ask you, "*What have you done with those offenses?*" I would like to share my thoughts with you on forgiveness this morning.

1. **Forgiveness is not a feeling, but a choice.** When others hurt us we have a choice of how we will respond. Very rarely will you ever feel like forgiving when you have been sinned against. It brings very strong emotions that we cannot deny. Anger is good, sin should make us angry. Jesus exhibited anger. The problem with anger is that if left alone it's considered murder. 1 John 3:15 tells us that, "*Anyone who hates a brother or sister is a murderer...*" Ephesians 4:26 says, "*In your anger do not sin.*" So I would suggest when you are angry, wait on the Lord on how to express it in a way that will bring about His purposes in a way that is redemptive.

2. **Realize how much you have been forgiven.** Unforgiveness is not even an option for the Christian way of life. "*For if you forgive other people when they sin against you, your heavenly Father will also forgive you*" (Matthew 6:14). Kids, all of us fail and it is good to remember we too have made terrible mistakes and are in much need of forgiveness.

3. **Know that Jesus understands.** This is always so helpful to me. Jesus was not someone who could not relate to what we go through. He was not someone who only told us what to do, but He showed us how by experiencing the same things Himself.

When I read how He was betrayed, mocked, spit on, despised, rejected, deserted, laughed at, striped, poked at, hit over and over again, and still chose the way of love…I am amazed. My thought this morning that broke my heart is that it was love that kept him on the cross for all the wrongs that people do. Our sins. His great pain. It is love that covers all our wrongs. *"Hatred stirs up conflict, but love covers over all wrongs"* (Proverbs 10:12).

4. **Forgiveness is a private matter.** Often when we are offended, we want to tell others, maybe to justify ourselves or make others dislike our offender. Forgiveness is giving up the right to hurt back. *"If your brother or sister sins, go and point out their fault, just between the two of you. If they listen to you, you have won them over. But if they will not listen to you, take one or two others along, so that 'every matter may be established by the testimony of two or three witnesses'"* (Matthew 18:15-16). This is important for the body of Christ because once you go destroying your offender's life, they may never recover and the body of Christ will be broken. This is grace and mercy. Resist the temptation to destroy. Remember love always builds up and we are called to this.

5. **Obedience is the key to forgiveness.** God's word asks us to do many things. These things are hard, if not impossible, but if we allow and believe that God's way is the only way, healing will be the result. It is a call to die to yourself and no one likes to die. Jesus speaks to us in Luke 6:27-28, *"Love your enemies, do good to those who hate you, bless those who curse you, pray for those who mistreat you."* Don't return evil for evil?! Mom, are you kidding?! No, I am not. Until you practice obedience you will not have peace. Again you will not feel like it. I think of the parable of the two sons. One was told to go to work in the field by his father and he told him, *"I will not!"* But later changed his mind and went. The other said, *"I will,"* but did not go. Which one of the two did what the father asked? The one who obeyed. I would say there is no life until you have died to your own. Dad and I

just read this in our devotions this morning in Matthew 10:39, *"Whoever finds their life will lose it, and whoever loses their life for my sake will find it."*

6. **Choose forgiveness over and over again.** Just when you think you get over one offense, something else comes up or a trigger will go off reminding you of an offense. In Matthew 18:21-22, Peter asked Jesus, *"Lord, how many times shall I forgive my brother or sister who sins against me? Up to seven times?' Jesus answered, 'I tell you, not seven times, but seventy-seven times.'"*

7. **Cancel the debt.** Jesus told a story of the unmerciful servant. Matthew 18:23-30 says,

> *"Therefore, the kingdom of heaven is like a king who wanted to settle accounts with his servants. As he began the settlement, a man who owed him ten thousand bags of gold was brought to him. Since he was not able to pay, the master ordered that he and his wife and his children and all that he had be sold to repay the debt. "At this the servant fell on his knees before him. 'Be patient with me,' he begged, 'and I will pay back everything.' The servant's master took pity on him, canceled the debt and let him go. "But when that servant went out, he found one of his fellow servants who owed him a hundred silver coins. "He grabbed him and began to choke him. 'Pay back what you owe me!' he demanded. His fellow servant fell to his knees and begged him, 'Be patient with me, and I will pay it back.' "But he refused. Instead, he went off and had the man thrown in prison until he could pay the debt."*

The moral of the story is to forgive the debts others owe you when they cannot pay it back. Sometimes people do things against you that they cannot ever pay back. You are like the banker, you hold the debt. Tear it up, Kids! You will never receive payment. Accept the joy of knowing you did as it has been done to you by God in Christ.

8. **Forgiveness is a road to healing.** Lewis B. Smedes once said, *"To forgive is to set a prisoner free and discover that the prisoner was you."* Deep hurt comes to those who have been sinned against. The deeper the wound the greater the pain. The enemy comes and tries to tell you that you have not forgiven because of all the feelings you are still working through. Truth is painful. It takes time. I think of when Grandpa had open heart surgery and his whole body was in shock. It took a really long time for him to heal. Some days, to him, it seemed like he would never get better or stop hurting. Then there were days that he got out of bed, began to take a couple of steps and gradually was able to do more and more. Then one day he was walking again. He had his setbacks, but he had great come backs as well. Why? Because he <u>wanted</u> to get better. He pressed through all of the pain and believed it was all for a better tomorrow. Today, he has only a scar representing what once was. There is no set time for healing, for God is the healer. Allow Him the time to heal you. *"He heals the brokenhearted and binds up their wounds"* (Psalm 147:3).

Love you all,

Mom

"Being Made Special"

Good Morning Children,

A family is made up of all unique and special members. I can recall times when special attention was given to one over the others. I think of the time when Jason was terribly sick in the hospital and at times I wondered if he would recover. My world stopped and all my attention was focused on him. It didn't mean I did not care about anyone else, but I knew if I did not care for him, our family would have never been the same. I remember special times when we celebrated the joys and successes of life: Marriages, babies, awards, birthdays and the like. I also remember the special times when we failed and worked on encouraging and strengthening one another. The family is ultimately important for strengthening and building up one another.

I was reading about the family of God this morning, to which all of us belong. I was challenged to ask, "What about when members of our family in the Lord are hurting?" "What about when they are weak?" "How can we help them?" In 1 Corinthians 12:12-31, Paul is teaching us that the body of Christ is made up of all kinds of different parts that make us one complete family. If I happen to be a foot, I cannot say to the hand that I don't need it. Or the eye cannot tell the hand that it doesn't need it, nor can the head say that to the feet. *"On the contrary, those parts that we think are less honorable we treat with **special** honor. And the parts that are unpresentable are treated with **special** modesty, while our presentable parts need no special treatment. But God has put the body together, giving greater honor to the parts that lacked it, so that there should be no division in the body, but that its parts should have equal* *concern for each other. If one part suffers, every part suffers with it; if one part is honored, every part rejoices with it"* (1 Corinthians 12:22-26).

Wouldn't it be wonderful if we really treated those who are in the family of God as a part of our own family? You know the ones whom we have hurt or the ones who have hurt you? If we didn't envy those who got special attention, but rejoiced with them? If one was without, we shared what we have? Paul goes on to tell them that he wants to show them a more excellent way to do this. He tells me, in the end of chapter 12 and beginning of chapter 13, that if I speak in tongues, have gifts of prophecy, fathom all the mysteries and process knowledge, have great faith, give all I have to the poor, surrender my body to flames, but If I do not love, I gain nothing!

Help us Lord, to pay **special** attention to those in our family that need to know that they matter, that they belong.

I love you all,

Mom

Jason and Joshua

"The Leader"

Good Morning Children,

"I'm following the leader, the leader, the leader. I'm following the leader, wherever he may go!"

The other night Joselyn was the leader. She was running as fast as she could through the house and it wasn't long before she had five other kids running behind her. She didn't ask anyone to join her. She was just doing what she enjoyed. Round and around they would go, laughing all the way, loving every minute. Joselyn is almost two and I thought, *"She gets it. She started doing something she loved and others just joined in."*

So often in the church it seems like we have to ask, drag and beg people to get involved. We hear a message of what we are supposed to do, how we are supposed to do it, and even where we are to do it, but the one telling us is not the one showing us or leading the way.

This made me think of why people followed Jesus. It's because his life was one of invitation. *"Come, follow me…Come with me!"* He would say. People were drawn to him like a magnet. Here was a man who was out there doing what he loved and others joined in. In that process he was leading people and showing them what to do and how to do it. He was a leader who led by example. I love what Paul wrote in 1 Corinthians 11:1, *"Follow my example, as I follow the example of Christ."* Watch me and then do as I do.

So my encouragement from Joselyn is to do what you enjoy. Be the example and then others will follow. Thanks Jos!

Love to you all,

Mom

Beverly and the kids in Africa

"Shattered Glass"

Good Morning Children,

Ever feel like throwing a glass on the wall just to see it shatter? Maybe you have felt that way inside. Something has been said or done and you feel hurt. Shattered. You want to run, but there is nowhere to run. You want to hide, but all the closets are full. Inside you are raging and want to respond, but instead you stuff all your feelings inside. I am sure we have all had those times.

When I was young and was taking care of my brothers, I used to bite my finger when I would get mad. It seemed to give me power; at least when I did it my brothers knew they better stop whatever they were doing to make me mad. In the process, my finger became very calloused and hard. Sometimes I would bite it so hard it would bleed and then I would have an ugly scab. Over the years it became numb and I didn't even feel the pain anymore. Although I haven't bitten it for years, I am still left with the scars of having done so.

In many ways, hurts are the same. If we hurt inside or we hurt others, our hearts become calloused and hard and sometimes even numb. Today I pray with all my heart that when times of trouble, hurt, disappointment, or disagreements come, and they will, that you will know how to handle them.

Do I know how to handle those times? Somewhat. Do I always succeed in handling those times well? Somewhat. But in all of those times the following are some of the things I strive for.

1. **Listen carefully.** James 1:19-20 states, *"Everyone should be quick to listen, slow to speak and slow to become angry, because human anger does not produce the righteousness that God desires."*

2. **Watch your word's for in them is life or death.** James 3:5-6 says, *"Likewise, the tongue is a small part of the body, but it makes great boasts. Consider what a great forest is set on fire by a small spark. The tongue also is a fire, a world of evil among the parts of the body. It corrupts the whole body, sets the whole course of one's life on fire, and is itself set on fire by hell."*
   James 3:9 states, *"With the tongue we praise our Lord and Father, and with it we curse human beings, who have been made in God's likeness. Out of the same mouth come praise and cursing. My brothers and sisters, this should not be."*

3. **Humble yourselves instead of elevating yourself. Put others before yourself.** James 4:6 tells us, *"But he gives us more grace. That is why the Scripture says: 'God opposes the proud but shows favor to the humble.'"*

4. **Submit yourselves to God.** James 4:7 says, *"Submit yourselves, then, to God. Resist the devil, and he will flee from you."*

5. **Ask for God's help.** James 1:5 tells us, *"If any of you lacks wisdom, you should ask God, who gives generously to all without finding fault…"*
   James 3:17 says, *"But the wisdom that comes from heaven is first of all pure; then peace-loving, considerate, submissive, full of mercy and good fruit, impartial and sincere."*

6. **Be patient with each other.** James 5:7-8 tells us, *"Be patient, then, brothers and sisters, until the Lord's coming. See how the farmer waits for the land to yield its valuable crop, patiently waiting for the autumn and spring rains. You too, be patient and stand firm, because the Lord's coming is near."*

7. **Be thankful and look for the good.** James 1:2-4 says, *"Consider it pure joy, my brothers and sisters, whenever you face trials of many kinds, because you know that the testing of your faith produces*

perseverance. Let perseverance finish its work so that you may be mature and complete, not lacking anything."

8. **Pray in the midst of your struggles.** James 5:13 says, *"Is anyone among you in trouble? Let them pray."*

I guess you can tell that James is my favorite book of the Bible. I once had the entire book memorized because it is so practical to everyday life. Kids, life is tough, but in God is true life.

Love,

Mom

P.S. I still have a full set of glassware in case you are wondering.

"Blessing God"

Good Morning Children,

I was asking Addi and Ayla this morning about how we bless God. Addi said we bless God when we are serving, praying, respecting, and honoring others. I asked them what those ideas looked like. They really didn't know what to say, so I read them the story Jesus told in Matthew 25 about blessing others.

The story Jesus told illustrated that we bless God when we do such things as giving others a drink when they are thirsty, food when they haven't eaten, or clothes when they need some. He said if we do these things we are actually doing it to Him. Blessing God is when we do what He asks. To further explain, I told them how it blesses their Mommy when she asks them to do something and they do it without complaining. Jesus also commanded us to be a blessing to others that talk bad about us or do things that hurt us. Blessing others is easy until it hurts or requires something from us, then it is hard. But those are the times we can bless God the most. It shows we really want to bless Him regardless of how we feel.

So my challenge to the girls was to find ways to bless God. Addi looked at Ayla when we finished and said, *"Would you like my orange juice?"* *"Yes I would,"* Ayla replied. To which I yelled, *"So you're blessing God, huh?"* They giggled. Ayla then asked me to play *"Old Maid."* *"Yes I will Ayla,"* I said. *"Blessing God, Nana?"* We giggled. Our morning was full of blessings.

Addi said this morning, *"We are a blessing to God when we are blessing others."*

Psalm 34:1 says, *"I will extol the Lord at all times; his praise will always be on my lips."* This is my prayer.

Love to all,

Mom

Addi and Ayla

"Needs"

Good Morning Children,

Often we come to the Lord in prayer with all of our needs or the needs of others. My question this morning is, *"Do we consider that the Lord has needs?"* How often do we say to the Lord, *"What are your needs today, Lord? How can I be of help or be of service to you?"* God allows us to engage in meeting His needs. In the story of the triumphal entry, Jesus uses two disciples to go and untie a donkey. If anyone wants to know why they are taking it, Jesus tells them to say, *"The Lord needs it"* (Luke 19:31).

I am sure the Lord doesn't need me, but I am honored by the fact that He chose me to be a part of meeting His needs. It may not be going to get a donkey, but it may be in giving to His children who need a kind word, a meal, or a blanket.

Today I pray we will all see the opportunities that the Lord has given to us.

Love you all,

Mom

"Whine or Shine"

Good Morning Children,

Philippians 2:14 tells us, *"Do everything without grumbling or arguing."* EVERYTHING?! Does that mean how I talk to my friends? Or even about my friends? How I work with people at my job? How I talk to my children or husband? How I serve my church or how I talk about my neighbor? Which of the two do you find you have trouble with the most?

Why do we complain? Complaining says we don't have something. For instance; position, things, respect…etc. Arguing? We argue because we want our way or we want to feel right. In either case we may feel attacked and respond by lashing out to defend ourselves.

I remember a good wakeup call your dad gave to me one day. I was complaining to him about him not doing something. After I had rattled on for a bit he looked at me and said, *"Sandy, do I do anything right?"* *"Yes,"* I said, *"You do so many things right."* He replied, *"Then tell me some of those things."*

In Philippians 2:14-16, Paul is drawing our attention to these two things and points out how we need to work them out of our life just as hard as we work at other things. These two affect everything we do and who we are. Verse 15 tells us why we should do this, *"so that you may become blameless and pure…Then you will shine among them like stars in the sky…"* I love to look at the stars on a clear night, the beauty is breathtaking! Kids, the fact is we live in a world that is filled with hatred and anger. However, our lives should say something different by the way we respond to life.

Complaining and arguing are things that happen on the inside of us. It is not just enough to try to stop arguing or complaining on the outside. By "working out" we should train ourselves to live a life of gratitude. Practice makes perfect!

It might be helpful to have a friend or partner hold you accountable in this area because sometimes we do it so much we don't even realize we are doing it. My conclusion is this. We can whine or shine.

This little light of mine. I'm gonna let it shine!

Shine on Kids!

Mom

"*Kindness*"

Good Morning Children,

Proverbs 14:31 says, "*Whoever oppresses the poor shows contempt for their Maker, but whoever is kind to the needy honors God.*"

In Africa they have a phrase, "*No one is left behind.*" I witnessed this truth yesterday. I picked up my mom to go to some neighborhood garage sales with Addi. We stepped out of the house and Addi took mom's arm and walked her to the car, opened the door and helped her in. Then, as soon as the car stopped she would assist mom in getting out. She would open the door, take her purse, grab her arm and help lift her out. After we were done at each sale location Addi would take the items my mom had purchased and carry them back to the car, open the door and stand waiting on her. This was her mission for the day. My mom was overwhelmed and kept saying how nice it was to be taken care of and how thoughtful and kind Addi was.

This was not something Addi had to do, it was something she enjoyed doing. No one had to tell her to do anything. Our natural instinct only thinks of itself, so I knew it was God in her wanting to express Himself through her in love. Although Addi was excited to discover what the sales locations had for her, what was most important to her that day was that her grandma was not left behind.

Isaiah 11:6 says, "*…a little child will lead them.*" Thanks Addi for leading the way!

Love to all,

Mom

"Treasures"

Good Morning Children,

"For where your treasure is, there your heart will be also" (Matthew 6:21).

Jesus warned us about not storing things up here. It's not that things are bad in themselves, but sometimes the things we have or want cause us to misplace our priorities and in the end they control us. Uncontrolled debt is one example of what happens when we focus on things. However, we are free to enjoy life when we are not preoccupied by things.

Recently I had a conversation with a 7 year old. Her father had just died suddenly and she was telling me of his death. She told me at the viewing of her father that people came and looked at him in the "treasure box". I asked her, *"A treasure box?"* She insisted her dad was in a treasure box. I loved it!

Kids, where do your treasures lie? You are my most precious treasures. Nothing is more important to me than my family. When I die all my things will be useless to me. The only lasting thing that will remain is what I have invested in you, the most important people in my life and knowing I made a difference in your life.

I love you beyond words; you are special, valued and worth more to me than anything.

Invest well,

Mom

"Do not store up for yourselves treasures on earth, where moths and vermin destroy, and where thieves break in and steal. But store up for yourselves treasures in heaven, where moths and vermin do not destroy, and where thieves do not break in and steal." Matthew 6:19-20

"*Looking for Jesus*"

Good Morning Children,

"And my God will meet all your needs according to the riches of his glory in Christ Jesus." Philippians 4:19

Ginny was telling us of a story about Belcer, a pastor in the worst part of Managua, Nicaragua. She said when he goes to the market, or just walking on the streets, people always come up to him with great needs. His response is almost always, *"Are you looking for Jesus?"* Belcer recognized he is not the one who can meet their needs. God uses him, but God has to be the source of peace for people. Jesus is the one who gives hope.

I pray each of you will seek God first when you have a need. God is faithful to show you the way.

I love you,

Mom

"*Beauty*"

Good Morning Children,

As I am here in Nicaragua I realize at times how overwhelming life can be. Our group witnessed a stabbing in front of a church where we serve. Jason held in his arms a little girl who was taken from her home, raped, and left for dead half buried next to a lake. She also had been missing for a month and a half. I witnessed three men just lying on the ground and I wondered if they were even alive. I visited a lady who lay dying and covered with flies. I know it broke my heart and I can only imagine how God feels. Yet in the very midst of it all, I also see beauty. All I have to do is look into the faces of the poor. God is among them, and I thank God He has allowed me to serve them in His name. I know each time we reach out to the poor we are an extension of His arms.

The Lord said in Matthew 25:35-40, *"For I was hungry and you gave me something to eat, I was thirsty and you gave me something to drink, I was a stranger and you invited me in, I needed clothes and you clothed me, I was sick and you looked after me, I was in prison and you came to visit me. Then the righteous will answer him, 'Lord, when did we see you hungry and feed you, or thirsty and give you something to drink? When did we see you a stranger and invite you in, or needing clothes and clothe you? When did we see you sick or in prison and go to visit you? The King will reply, 'Truly I tell you, whatever you did for one of the least of these brothers and sisters of mine, you did for me.'"*

Be used of God. It is by far the greatest thing you will ever experience.

Father, use my children in ways that they will be able to bless others.

Hugs,

Mom

"*Overcoming*"

Good Morning Children,

Today I would like to share my thoughts on the power of positive thinking. To me it is the single most effective tool I have in my life. Practicing it has made me an over-comer of the negative words and thoughts that have been spoken over me. I have chosen to believe God's word about <u>who</u> I am, rather than who others <u>think</u> I am.

I have memorized these scriptures as they have helped me with this:

"For as a person thinks in his heart, so is he." Proverbs 23:7, King James Version

"…we take captive every thought to make it obedient to Christ." 2 Corinthians 10:5

"Finally, brothers and sisters, whatever is true, whatever is noble, whatever is right, whatever is pure, whatever is lovely, whatever is admirable – if anything is excellent or praiseworthy – think about such things." Philippians 4:8

More and more each day I try to live by thinking positively, by finding the good in all people. The ones who seem to be the worst are the ones who need love the most. You can make a difference by finding the good. I write this to you today because there is nothing you cannot do if you put your mind to it. Does it take hard work? Yes, but if you want something you can achieve it. Speak words of life instead of death. I pray God will empower you with faith to believe anything is possible.

I believe in each of you!

Mom

"God is Able"

Good Morning Children,

God is ABLE. Did you hear me? GOD IS ABLE! Believing in God is believing when we cannot see the light at the end of a tunnel.

One time several years ago your dad and I were going through rough times. He went out and purchased a birdfeeder and seed and placed it in front of a big window we had in our house. I asked him, *"Doug, why did you go buy a bird feeder and food when we can hardly buy food for ourselves?"* He replied, *"Because it will serve as a reminder that God is able to meet all our needs. I will feed the birds and God will feed us."*

God is and was faithful to us. Many times when people I know are struggling I buy them a birdfeeder and some seed to remind them of God's faithfulness.

Jesus said in Luke 12:22-24, *"Then Jesus said to his disciples: 'Therefore I tell you* [Chris, Bev, Jason and Josh] *do not worry about your life, what you will eat; or about your body, what you will wear. For life is more than food, and the body more than clothes. Consider the ravens: They do not sow or reap, they have no storeroom or barn; yet God feeds them. And how much more valuable you are than birds!"*

You are valuable Kids. God loves you and if you never had trials your faith wouldn't grow. Dad and I have learned and are still learning each day how to trust God more and more.

Believe He is able!

Love,

Mom

"God's Handprints"

Good Morning Children,

"…it was not you who sent me here, but God." Genesis 45:8

I've been reading about Joseph who was sold by his brothers into slavery because they were jealous of him. They told his father, who loved him dearly, that he had died. Because Joseph honored God, he would not sleep with his master's wife, so she had him put into prison. Even then God had a plan for Joseph. During this time in his life the Bible says, *"the Lord was with him; he showed him kindness and granted him favor in the eyes of the prison warden"* (Genesis 39:21).

The point is, Kids, your life belongs to God, no matter what happens. God will use it to fulfill His plans for you. As I review the life of your dad and me, I can see the handprint of God now. During those difficult times, I wondered where He was or if we'd missed something God was trying to teach us. Sometimes God takes you to a place in life to prepare you for the next place. It is a journey. I believe that is why we should be thankful knowing God is designing our lives and building character in us. Joseph was able to recognize God's hand and was able to save his whole family.

Many are God's plans for you Kids. His love for you is perfect. Seek to serve Him and you will learn of His mercies and goodness. I am thankful to be alive today to see God working in each of you. I am thankful I am married to a man who has taught me so much about God and led us as a family in a life of faith.

Praying for you,

Mom

"Faithfulness Gains Respect"

Good Morning Children,

My aunt Martha Jane, my father's sister, died on April 4ᵗʰ at the age of 88. She had Alzheimer's and couldn't remember anything or anyone during the last seven years of her life. Her husband of sixty-seven years cared for her each day even though his health was failing as well. Towards the end of his life he lay very sick in the hospital. When his wife Martha Jane died he asked to be taken in an ambulance and wheeled in on a stretcher, accompanied by his sons to their mother's funeral to say goodbye.

My father's brother, Uncle Don spoke of his sister at the funeral. He told the story of how, when his sister was ill and incoherent and even though he was a doctor and a very busy man, he found time to travel nine hours away to visit his sister while she was sick. People who worked for him asked why he would do that since she had no idea of who he was. He told them, *"She may not remember who I am, but I remember who she is."* Then he spoke of his love for her. Two weeks later, Uncle Bill died and went to be with Martha Jane.

As I thought of their lives, I was honored to be a part of this family. Their love had lasted a lifetime. *"Until death do us part."* I am very proud of them. Again, Kids, faithfulness gains respect.

"For the Lord is good and his love endures forever; his faithfulness continues through all generations." Psalm 100:5

Those who follow after you will remember you for your
_____. You fill in the blank.

I love you,

Mom

Christopher and son Kellan (Born 7/14/14).

If you have any questions or comments for the author, you are welcome to do so at goodmorningchildren61@gmail.com.

Printed in the United States
By Bookmasters